AUTHOR

Eduardo Manuel Gil Martínez (25 June 1970) is a historian and has been passionate about Spanish history for several years, mainly about the Second World War and the age of the Reconquista. Author of numerous texts on the Second World War for Spanish and Italian magazines such as 'Revista Española de Historia Militar', AMARTE, 'Ritterkreuz' or 'The Axis Forces in the Second World War 1939-1945'. In addition to the title we publish, he is also the author of: "Sevilla Reina y Mora. Historia del reino independiente sevillano. Siglo XI', 'Breslau 1945. El último bastión del Reich', 'The Spaniards in the SS and the Wehrmacht. 1944-45. The Ezquerra unit in the Battle of Berlin ", The Bulgarian Air Force in World War II. The forgotten ally of Germany', 'Romanian Armoured Forces in the Second World War', 'Hungarian Armoured Forces in the Second World War', 'Spanish Air Force in the Second World War', 'Hispano Aviación Ha-1112' (about the last Messerschmitt 109 ever built in Spain) and other texts for important publishers such as Almena, Kagero, Schiffer and Pen & Sword.

Juan Arráez Cerdá is a Spanish Aviation expert and owner of one of the best pictures' collections of Spanish Aviation. He is the author of many books and articles about Aviation (in French and Spanish).

PHOTO AKNOWLEDGEMENT:
LET: LUIS EUGENIO TOGORES
CCJ: CARLOS CABALLERO JURADO POR MEDIO DE JUAN ARRÁEZ CERDÁ
NEG: NEGREIRA POR MEDIO DE JUAN ARRÁEZ CERDÁ
BIBLIOTECA VIRTUAL DE DEFENSA (BVD)
JUAN ARRÁEZ CERDÁ (JAC).

PUBLISHING'S NOTES

None of unpublished images or text of our book may be reproduced in any format without the expressed written permission of Luca Cristini Editore (already Soldiershop.com) when not indicate as marked with license creative commons 3.0 or 4.0. Luca Cristini Editore has made every reasonable effort to locate, contact and acknowledge rights holders and to correctly apply terms and conditions to Content. Every effort has been made to trace the copyright of all the photographs. If there are unintentional omissions, please contact the publisher in writing at: info@soldiershop.com, who will correct all subsequent editions.

Our trademark: Luca Cristini Editore©, and the names of our series & brand: Soldiershop, Witness to war, Museum book, Bookmoon, Soldiers&Weapons, Battlefield, War in colour, Historical Biographies, Darwin's view, Fabula, Altrastoria, Italia Storica Ebook, Witness To History, Soldiers, Weapons & Uniforms, Storia etc. are herein © by Luca Cristini Editore.

LICENSES COMMONS

This book may utilize part of material marked with license creative commons 3.0 or 4.0 (CC BY 4.0), (CC BY-ND 4.0), (CC BY-SA 4.0) or (CC0 1.0). We give appropriate attribution credit and indicate if change were made in the acknowledgments field. Our WTW books series utilize only fonts licensed under the SIL Open Font License or other free use license.

For a complete list of Soldiershop titles please contact Luca Cristini Editore on our website: www.soldiershop.com or www.cristinieditore.com. E-mail: info@soldiershop.com

IN MEMORIAM: Eduardo Gil and Juan Arráez

Title: **SPANISH VOLUNTEERS IN GERMANY DURING WORLD WAR II - VOL. 1**
Code.: **WTW-058 EN** by Juan Arráez Cerdá and Eduardo Manuel Gil Martínez
ISBN code: 9791255891192 first edition May 2024
Language: English. Size: 177,8x254mm. Cover & Art Design: Luca S. Cristini

WITNESS TO WAR (SOLDIERSHOP) is a mark of Luca Cristini Editore, via Orio, 33/D - 24050 Zanica (BG) ITALY.

WITNESS TO WAR

SPANISH VOLUNTEERS IN GERMANY DURING WORLD WAR II - VOL. 1
WEHRMACHT, WAFFEN SS & SD

PHOTOS & IMAGES FROM WORLD WARTIME ARCHIVES

JUAN ARRÁEZ CERDÁ
EDUARDO MANUEL GIL MARTÍNEZ

BOOKS TO COLLECT

CONTENTS

PREFACE..5
POLITICAL RELATIONS BETWEEN SPAIN AND GERMANY DURING WORLD WAR II..9
THE BLUE DIVISION (1941-1943)..17
    Formation...17
    Deployment..27
    Leningrad Front: Novgorov..27
    Volkhov River Front...28
    The Ilmen Lake achievement..47
    The battle of Krasny Bor...52
    Repatriation...81
BIBLIOGRAPHY...96

▲ A phalangist volunteer manifestation to fight against the Soviet Union (JAC).

PREFACE

During the Second World War, Spain did not take part as a Nation, although many Spaniards did take part in it, both on one side and on the other.

After the Spanish Civil War, Francisco Franco's regime was indebted both morally and materially to Adolf Hitler's Germany and Benito Mussolini's Italy, which, together with the affinity for these governments, led to efforts to align Spain within the Axis.

Since the situation in Spain after three years of war was not at all adequate to face new confrontations and that Francisco Franco was aware of this, such an alliance was never reached.

The fact of the invasion of the Soviet Union by the Axis troops, gave rise to the Spanish government to meet the demand of many ex-combatants, as well as young people who did not have the opportunity to fight in the Spanish Civil War to continue the fight against communism that had already begun in the Spanish confrontation.

This clamor was transformed into the División Española de Voluntarios (DEV) or Spanish Division of Volunteers, which has come to be popularly known as the División Azul (DA) or Blue Division. As the recruits for it, volunteers to fight against the Soviets, they were largely people with strong ideological convictions, which made them behave with immeasurable drive and courage when it came to fighting, despite the complicated situation they had to face on the Soviet northern front.

But the situation of the Second World War and the strong pressure from the Allies to withdraw the Spanish troops under the command of the Germans, led the Spanish government to consider the possibility of repatriating the Blue Division (integrated into the German land army) and the Blue Squadron (which was integrated into the German air forces).

Among the pressures that led to the withdrawal of the Blue Division in November 1943 was the threat by the Allies to invade the Canary Islands. But as the circumstances were politically complex enough to maintain a balance between the Axis and the Allies, and there was a firm will of thousands of divisionaries not to leave their comrades fighting against the Soviets in the lurch, this retreat was made in two stages. Initially, the Blue Division withdrew, and its last action of the war took place on 5 October, the same day it was ordered to leave the front and then be repatriated to Spain. She was officially disbanded on 17 November and her last batch left the Eastern Front on 24 December 1943. When the DA marched, some 2,200 men were still integrated into the structure of the German army, which was called the Spanish Legion of Volunteers (LEV) or more popularly known as the Blue Legion, under the orders of Colonel Navarro. On November 17, General Esteban-Infantes signed the order that gave birth to the LEV. This Legion was incorporated into the German 121st Infantry Division.

But the Allied pressure could not allow this studied "double face" of the Spanish government, so contacts with the Spanish authorities multiplied, pressuring them even more, to the point that the Legion had to be withdrawn from the front, repatriating its men to Spain. On March 17 the return began: the Engineer Unit began the march, followed by other small units. The first train of soldiers arrived at the Spanish border on March 28 and the last on April 11, 1944. Thus, on April 12, 1944, we already found the members of the Blue Legion in Spanish territory. All that remained to be done was small groups that had been tasked with finalizing all the documentation, liquidating the surplus material and repatriating the Spaniards hospitalized in the hospitals of Königsberg and Riga; Although, as we shall see, this was not exactly the case.

▲ The doctor examines the Blue Division volunteers. PUBLIC DOMAIN.

▼ The number of volunteers for the Blue Division was much higher than necessary (BVD).

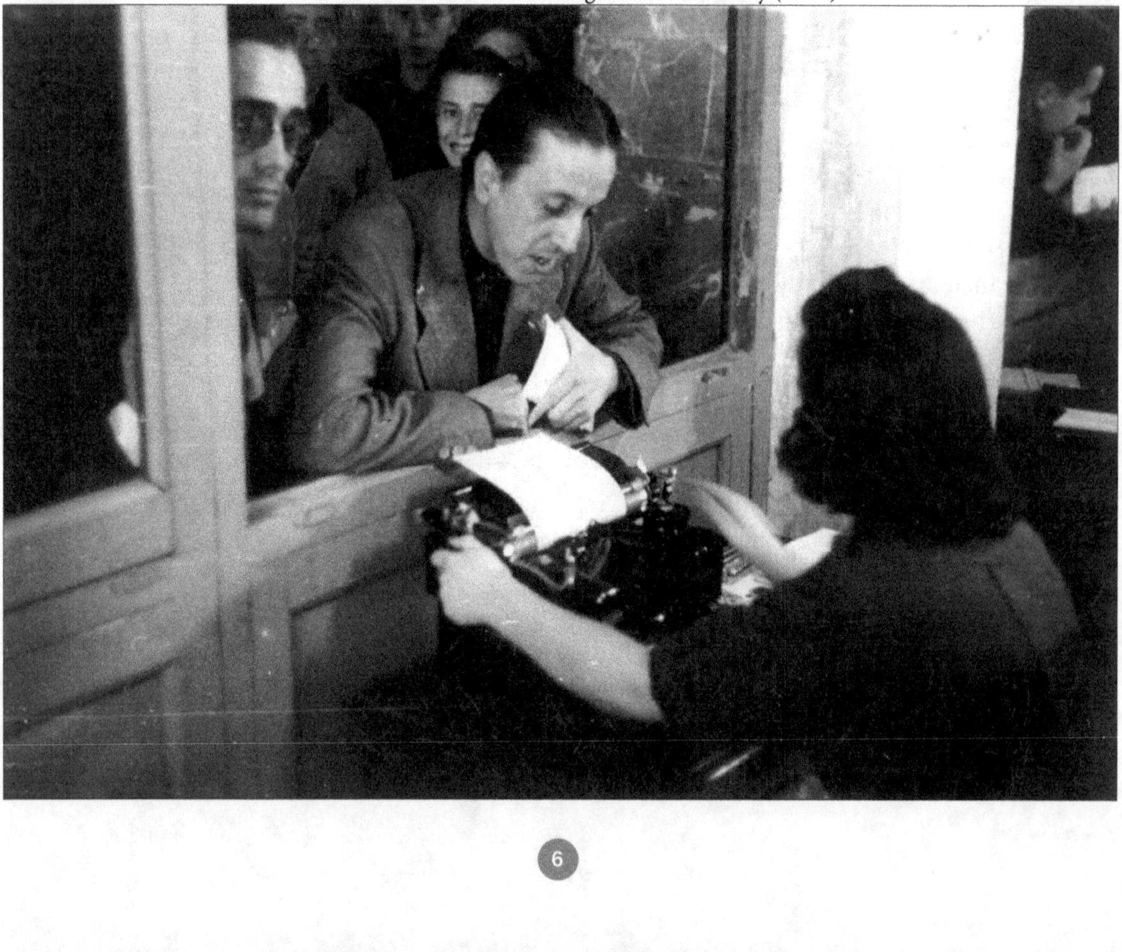

▲ Photograph of Colonel Rodrigo reviewing the volunteers of the Blue Division (BVD).

▼ A formation of Spanish soldiers during an exercise. Many of them had fought in the Spanish Civil War and were real veterans (BVD).

▲ One of the Spanish soldiers on their way to Germany (BVD).

POLITICAL RELATIONS BETWEEN SPAIN AND GERMANY DURING WORLD WAR II

To learn more about this topic, it is advisable to read the interesting articles by Gómez and Sacristán, on which we structure this chapter.

Following the end of the Spanish Civil War, Francisco Franco became the head of the Spanish state. The important help it had received during that conflict from Germany and Italy, meant that the Spanish regime was very "close" to that of both countries, which could be considered the greatest examples of the new authoritarian system in Europe and that each day that passed were acquiring more power within the European map. Not surprisingly, Spain had an important debt, and not only a moral one, to Hitler's Germany and Mussolini's Italy, since it was now demanding payment for the military, economic, political and diplomatic aid they had received that facilitated their victory.

The total amount of the debts that Spain had with the Government of Italy amounted to more than 7,000 million lire, although they were reduced to about 5,000 million by order of Benito Mussolini, in exchange for obtaining important economic benefits from Italy in Spain. Finally, after the corresponding diplomatic meetings, it was agreed to establish a payment schedule that would begin in 1942 (and end on June 30, 1967). With regard to the debt with Germany, Spain's situation was clearly inferior, having to be forced to allow German companies to enter the Spanish economy. With regard to the monetary debt contracted, diplomatic meetings were also held that prolonged the solution to the payment of the same, so that the end of the Second World War saw how Spain, after having made very few payments, unilaterally cancelled this obligation in 1945.

The new Spanish state, which emerged from the Civil War, needed to "formalize" its situation worldwide while showing its political inclination. He began by signing a treaty of friendship with Portugal, aware of this country's pro-British leanings. As early as March 1939, the Spanish government signed a treaty of friendship with Germany requiring mutual consultation in the event of an attack on either country. This pact left Spain in a lower position than Germany, with which it was associated. Spain also adhered to the Anti-Comintern Pact, which focused on communism, but with few specific obligations to fulfil. On 8 May, the Government of Spain officially withdrew from the League of Nations in Geneva.

The beginning of the Second World War, with Germany's action on Poland, began a new era in Spain's international relations. When on September 3, 1939, Britain and France declared war on Germany, Franco on behalf of the Spanish government made a public appeal to reconsider the situation and resume negotiations. Likewise, the Spanish Minister of Foreign Affairs, Colonel Juan Beigbeder, informed the German Government of the impossibility of holding negotiations for a Spanish-German cultural agreement. The situation was complex, since there was indeed a great political and ideological affinity for the Axis powers, but the Western Allied powers were closer to Spain and its North African territories with the consequent danger of a severe "blockade" led by Great Britain. These facts, together with the ruinous situation of Spain after the very recent fratricidal war and with the evident exhaustion of the population, determine that the Government of Spain decides on a third possibility, which is that of neutrality in the world conflict, the same position it had during the First World War. On September 4, 1939, a decree was established in the Official State Gazette officially proclaiming neutrality, which read as follows:

"The state of war which, by misfortune, exists between England. France and Poland, on the one hand, and Germany, on the other, hereby order the strictest neutrality of Spanish nationals, in accordance with the laws in force and the principles of public international law.
—Burgos, September 4, 1939. Year of the Victory.
– Francisco Franco.
– The Minister of Foreign Affairs, Juan Beigbeder y Atienza."

In this way, the atmosphere of intimacy of the Spaniards came to an end. The editorial of ABC (Spanish newspaper) of that day said, among other things: "This attitude represents, on the one hand, the magnificent initiation of an international policy on the basis of the strictest independence, and on the other, the logical consequence of the impulses of reconstruction that are currently moving Spain."

With regard to our "real" possibilities in the event of a military intervention, it should be noted that the Spanish Army, although "tired" and with weapons that were quickly becoming obsolete, was numerically important and had great experience in combat. Regarding the latter, it should be said that this armament that Italy and Germany had supplied to Franco's army was very advanced and of the first order during the period of the Spanish conflict; It was becoming obsolete very quickly. We remember that the most modern armored vehicle of the Spanish army after the end of the Civil War were the T-26 of Soviet origin and the PzKw I of German origin, apparently outdated in 1940.

This declaration of Spain's neutrality allowed the Germans to act with the peace of mind that Spain would not serve as an area of operations for the Western Allies. In the same way, the powerful German Army, sure of its superiority, would not need the exhausted Spanish Army for any of its offensive operations in Europe, it would be enough to have it as a "friend".

Between May and June 1940, France was overwhelmed by the unstoppable advance of the invincible German Army. The Government of Spain observes with great admiration the events in France, with the increase in Germanophilia in our country. This admiration in a certain way overturned the direction of the Spanish government, since until then it had more to Italy as a reference than to Germany. On June 3, 1940, Francisco Franco had already sent Adolf Hitler a letter in which he stated that he was ready to provide him at any time with the services he considered most necessary.

In mid-June 1940, the highest political and military authorities in Spain tried to side with the winner. Due to this old relationship between Germany and Spain, the idea of being part of the new victorious order and of reviving the old laurels of the Spanish empire in northwest Africa is raised. Days before the French capitulation to Germany, Spain changed its status from neutrality to non-belligerence: This new positioning within Spain's international order would allow Franco's government to show its support and identification with the Axis powers.

Relations began to be established between Madrid and Berlin for purely warmongering purposes. So "strong" men in Spain such as Ramón Serrano Súñer, Dionisio Ridruejo or Antonio Tovar (both linked to the propaganda system of the Franco regime) negotiated the use of Spain as a base of action for the so-called "Operation Phoenix" with which the occupation of the enclave of Gibraltar was intended, preventing the hegemony that the British had at the air and naval level in Mediterranean (in this case western) waters. In the same way, a new front would be opened for the conduct of military operations in North Africa.

The Spanish pretensions in the event of entering the War with the Axis were very clear, since Gibraltar would once again be under Spanish sovereignty, but the territories that would be taken in that hypothetical intervention in North Africa, Algeria and French Morocco would also become dependent on our country. Spanish expansion would also materialize towards the increase of territory in Río de Oro and the Gulf of Guinea.

These issues between Spain and Germany required a greater push, so it was decided to arrange a meeting between the two senior leaders of the respective countries. Thus, after a visit by Himmler, head of the Gestapo, to Madrid, and the visit on September 13, 1940 of Serrano Suñer as Minister of the Interior and Interior to meet with Hitler in Berlin; and later, on the 16th, with Von Ribbentrop (who was the one who came to receive him at the Anhalter station) it was agreed that it was necessary to hold a meeting at the summit of the two leaders. As a result of this interest on both sides, the Hendaye meeting between Francisco Franco and Adolf Hitler took place on October 23, 1940; They were accompanied by their respective Ministers of Foreign Affairs, Serrano Suñer on the Spanish side and Von Ribbentrop on the German side, who drafted the protocol contemplating Spain's participation in the war in exchange for the aforementioned territorial compensations (which has been called the Protocol of Hendaye). Between Hitler's doubts about the possible support that Spain's contribution to the war would mean, the requests on the part of the Spanish side that clashed in many cases with the pretensions of Vichy France (a German ally) and the situation created in the Balkans due to the defeat of the Italian army in Greece in October 1940; In the end, Spain did not take the step to become an ally of Germany. Despite this, during the meeting the aforementioned Protocol of Hendaye was signed, in which Spain undertook to enter the war with Germany when it had satisfied the territorial demands in North

Africa. Another of the agreements reached in the Hendaye interview was the creation of a corps of Spanish "volunteers" who would be incorporated into the German army in the event of a military operation against the Soviet Union.

Finally, the only territory that Spain took during the world conflict was the city of Tangier in 1940, arguing that after the fall of France this city had become ungovernable. In 1945, Spain left the city, declaring it an open city again. Hitler was greatly relieved by this fact.

On November 19, 1940, Hitler, in an interview with Serrano Suñer in Berlin, asked for a date for Spain's entry into the war and the beginning of the siege of Gibraltar. The Spaniard eternalizes the answer by acknowledging important Spanish logistical problems for this purpose. Faced with Spain's delay in intervening, Germany asked for permission for troops to pass through Spanish territory in order to attack Gibraltar. On December 11, 1940, Spain rejected the request, arguing that it was impossible for Spain to maintain sovereignty over Spanish Guinea and the Canary Islands. In addition, the excuse of the lack of preparation of the Spanish Army was also put forward, as well as the need to receive significant quantities of both transport material and the need to receive a considerable amount of grain beforehand.

Franco's subsequent interviews with the leaders of Italy and Vichy France; with Mussolini in Bordighera and with Petain in Montpellier in February 1941, they did not change Spain's position in the conflict in any respect.

On June 21, 1941, German troops made a surprise attack on the Soviet Union, producing a sense of euphoria in much of Europe. In Spain, the regime's top leaders mostly identify with this new enemy of Germany's friendly people. It was not for nothing that the Soviet Union had been the main support of the Republican Army during the Spanish Civil War. In Spain, there are various speeches and rallies that ask to participate in the struggle against communism, embodied by the Soviet enemy as he considers it largely to blame for our Civil War. Officially, the Spanish government heeded the popular outcry and allowed the organization of volunteer companies (largely Falangists) to help Germany on the Eastern front.

Finally, the Spanish Volunteer Division was created, which under the command of Agustín Muñoz Grandes left for the Russian front in August 1941.

But the World War from 1942 onwards began to give major setbacks to the German Army; the summer offensive in the Caucasus was halted at the end of September and the terrible carnage of the Battle of Stalingrad or the Allied landing in Casablanca in November 1942 began. On February 17, 1942, the meeting in Seville between Franco and Oliveira Salazar took place in which the Iberian Pact was signed, which meant a rapprochement with Portugal, which despite its fascist regime continued to maintain close relations with the United Kingdom historically. On November 8, 1942, a letter from Roosevelt to Franco was delivered by the United States ambassador informing him of the occupation of French possessions in North Africa and guaranteeing the neutrality and integrity of Spanish territory. Franco therefore received important Allied pressures that forced Spanish foreign policy to maintain a rather ambiguous balance in order to "satisfy" both sides as much as possible; On September 3, 1942, Serrano Suñer was replaced in the Ministry of Foreign Affairs by Francisco Gómez Jordana, considered closer to the Western Allies than his predecessor.

Supplies provided in Spanish territory are limited to both Italian and German aircraft and ships; but on the other hand, agreements were signed for the shipment of food and raw materials to the Third Reich.

During 1943 continues the decline of German power in Europe and North Africa; a situation that does not help at all the situation of equilibrium maintained by the Government of Spain.

So, it has to accept the only way out, under Anglo-American pressure, which is to return to its initial position of neutrality; This became effective on October 3 (some sources say 1) October 1943. In the same way, the repatriation of the members of the Spanish Volunteer Division would begin in December of that year. But the Allies will continue their pressure on Spain to cut off the supply of various materials to Germany, including tungsten.

Spain, or rather, Franco's policy continues to be torn between the pressures of the Allies and their pro-Germanism. Food and raw materials, especially tungsten (essential for advanced precision engineering and armaments production), iron, zinc, lead and mercury, continue to be shipped to Germany. On October 25, 1943, the U.S. government demanded that Spain impose a total embargo on tungsten exports to the Axis, under threat of cutting off oil supplies, temporarily suspending oil shipments to Spain in January 1944. This situation would lead to the collapse of the Spanish State, so on May 2, 1944, tungsten exports to Germany ended (although possibly some minimal quantities continued to arrive until August of the same year), German agents were expelled from Tangier, the Japanese mission in Spain was closed, and a commitment was made to collaborate with the United States and Great Britain on military matters. A few months later, planes from the U.S. Air Transport Command received authorization to refuel in Spanish territory.

On 12 April 1945, with the war in Europe almost over, Spain broke off diplomatic relations with Japan. At the end of the world war, Spain found itself in a difficult situation, as the victors continued to consider it a government with a clear fascist tendence.

▲ Map of the train journey made by the first expeditions of the Blue Division between Spain and the Grafenwöhr military camp in Germany in the summer of 1941. By FoxR.

▲ Volunteers of the Blue Division showing their German comrades the battalion pennant with the precious imperial coat of arms, the work of sisters and brides (BVD).

▼ The salute of the soldiers of the Blue Division after a meal in the courtyard of the Mola Military Hospital before departure Marín-Kutxa Fototeka Fund.

▲ Some Spanish soldiers fraternise with a German soldier in a bar during the journey from Madrid to Grafenwöhr (JAC).

▼ Four Blue Division soldiers in German uniform and red beret talk casually with a Red Cross nurse in Grafenwöhr. July 1941. PUBLIC DOMAIN.

▲ Photograph of Blue Division volunteers marching to the Polish front.

▼ Training Spanish soldiers in the Reich, without having changed their uniforms yet.

▲ Troops of the Spanish Volunteer Division, predecessor of the Blue Legion, defend a position. Due to the growing Soviet power, the Spanish troops had to remain on the defensive on many occasions. Public domain.

▼ Some soldiers of the Spanish Volunteer Division during an exercise. The harshness of the fighting would demonstrate the high degree of skill, training and courage of the Spanish soldiers during their time in the Soviet Union. Public domain.

THE BLUE DIVISION (1941-1943)

As we have mentioned before, the so-called Blue Division arose as a response to the popular clamor of part of the citizenry who, after the attack of the German army on the U.S.S.R. in June 1941, showed with a large demonstration in Madrid orchestrated mainly by the Falange (a fascist party), the desire to fight the Soviets in their own country. To repay them for the visit they had made by supporting the Republican side during the Spanish Civil War, while returning the favor and partially paying off the debt contracted with Germany for their support of the national side in that war. It was during this demonstration that Serrano Suñer, Minister of Foreign Affairs and President of the Political Board of the Falange, delivered his well-known speech from one of the balconies of the headquarters of the General Secretariat of the Movement:
"Comrades, this is not the time for speeches; but it is true that the Falange is now issuing its condemnatory sentence: Russia is guilty, guilty of our Civil War. Guilty of the death of José Antonio, our founder. And of the death of so many comrades and so many soldiers who fell in that war due to the aggression of Russian communism. The extermination of Russia is a requirement of the history and future of Europe..."
Due to the great popular enthusiasm that was generated, with little effort it was possible to recruit its members from among the military and thousands of volunteers who were ready to give their names in the recruitment offices that were created for that purpose. Among these volunteers, there were some military men who had not fought in the Spanish Civil War and wanted to prove to themselves and their comrades that they were capable of going to the front. It is said that some young officers fresh out of the Academy, faced with the prospect of a war in the world, did not consent to let this opportunity pass them by. Also, in young university students with a desire for adventure, or with the romantic ideal of defending convictions such as God and country, the idea of enlistment in the Spanish Division of Volunteers caught on strongly.
The Spanish situation that was decreed at the beginning of the world conflict was one of neutrality despite the fact that a good part of the Germanophile population existed; In this decree it was commented that "the state of war that unfortunately exists between England, France and Poland on the one hand, and Germany, on the other, is officially recorded, the strictest neutrality is hereby ordered to the Spanish subjects". On June 12, 1940, it adopted the situation of "non-belligerence", in a similar way to what Italy did before joining the armed conflict. Despite this first step that Spain took by getting closer to Germany, the negotiations for Spain's entry into the war carried out with Von Ribbentrop did not culminate in the union of Spain to the Axis due to a lack of understanding (voluntary or not) on both sides. For this reason, the situation in which Spain found itself *vis-à-vis* Germany was quite complex. The fact of the invasion of the Soviet Union made it possible to relieve the pressure that Adolf Hitler was exerting on Francisco Franco, by sending an expeditionary force to Russia. This step was considered by the Germans at first as a first step for Spain's gradual entry into the war.

Formation

The announcement of the recruitment to be part of the Division that was going to fight against communism in Russia had a quick and enthusiastic response, queues forming at the hitch pennants created in all the Spanish provinces and in the then Spanish Morocco.
The guidelines for their induction indicated that recruits were enlisted for the duration of the campaign. The unit created was officially called the Spanish Division of Volunteers and this is stated in all official Spanish documentation, but despite this the unit was and continues to be popularly called Blue Division. Their command would be in the hands of the Army and absolutely all Officers with employment higher than Ensign would come from the Army, although the Falangists who had been Provisional Ensigns during the Civil War could maintain their rank. As for the sergeants, two-thirds would come from the Army and the remaining third from the FE-J.O.N.S. Militias (Falange Española de las Juntas de Ofensiva Nacional Sindicalista or Spanish Falange of National Unionist Offensive Boards). However, it should be noted that a large number of officers and non-commissioned officers were also Falangists.
The head of the Division was appointed by Major General Agustín Muñoz Grandes, a seasoned and effective veteran of the campaigns in Morocco and the Civil War, and who was also a Falangist (a member of Falange).

On July 5, a Spanish Commission flew to Germany in order to coordinate the dispatch of the Blue Division. On their arrival they were surprised to find that the Wehrmacht Divisions had three Infantry Regiments, while the Spanish Infantry had four. Consequently, the Spanish Division consisted of 640 chiefs and officers and 2,272 non-commissioned officers and 15,780 soldiers, while the German Division consisted of 526, 2,813 and 14,397 respectively. As a result, the Spaniard had too many chiefs and officers, no non-commissioned officers, and the number of soldiers exceeded 1,200, which astonished the Spaniards, who had not been previously informed of it.

Faced with the impossibility of repatriating the surplus personnel for political reasons, it was decided that a reserve should be formed with it in order to cover the casualties suffered.

Finally, the Germans confirmed that the Reich would bear all the expenses of the Division from the day it crossed the border into France. Soldiers would receive their pay from the moment they crossed the French border. There would also be a combat bonus, family allowance, hospitalization and postal franchise to the Spanish border. The Wehrmacht would supply all armaments, ammunition and supplies. Military justice would be applied according to the Spanish military code, although German would prevail when Spanish soldiers were temporarily stationed under German command. The uniform of the Blue Division would be the German one, but it would have a shield on the right sleeve of the warrior with the Spanish colors red-yellow-red and the legend SPAIN.

Finally, on the night of July 12, everything was ready for the 19 railway convoys to leave Germany the next day, transporting the 17,294 Spaniards who were preparing to start a great adventure. Thus, on the afternoon of July 13, an immense crowd of Madrileños (citizens from Madrid) crowded the huge Estación del Norte (North Rail station), as well as the entrance square and the surrounding streets, while shouts of "Viva Franco" and "Arriba España" thundered while a Music Band tried to make itself heard over the noise of the crowd. Then, with a loud whistle from the locomotive, it started while thousands of voices began the chant of the "Cara al Sol" (a falangist hymn).

The journey through occupied France was, for the various convoys, cold and with minor incidents as they observed how at the stations some Frenchmen and exiled Spaniards raised their fists as they passed. But when they crossed the Rhine and entered Germany, things changed completely, and so when they arrived in Karlsrhue they were greeted by an enthusiastic crowd of more than 10,000 people.

When the Spanish contingents began to arrive at Grafenwöhr, they received the news that there was a surplus of a Regiment and also that the Division would not be motorized as had been thought, since like all German infantry divisions it would be equipped with carts and horses. Thus, it turned out that for each driver five riders had to be enabled, while the mounted part of the Division that had recruited riders would receive motorcycles. On the other hand, the Artillery, which only had drivers, would have to make do with horses and also the Reconnaissance Group, which was prepared to use horses, would be riding bicycles.

General Muñoz Grandes told his Colonels that he was going to disband the Rodrigo Regiment, but that this Colonel would be the Chief of the Infantry and 2nd Chief of the Division, so the rest of the Colonels: Pimentel, Vierna and Esparza, were happy to continue in command of their regiments. As for Rodrigo's Battalions, they would be distributed among the other Regiments, so there would be no repatriation as had been feared. In addition to its Battalions, each Regiment had a Cycling Company, an Artillery Support Company, an Anti-Tank Company and a Staff with an Assault Section.

The Wehrmacht assigned the 250th for the Spanish Division, so it was named Infanterie Division 250 and its regiments were numbered 262 for the Pimentel, 263 for the Vierna and 269 for the Esparza. From 29 September of the same year, they fought as part of the German 16th Army in Army Group North.

The Blue Division was somewhat different from the German divisions, as it was difficult to appoint a second in command and also to be the commander of the infantry. On the other hand, since there were no replacement troops at the front, a reserve battalion was organized with three rifle companies, a battalion that was soon known by the Guripas (soldiers) with the peculiar name of "Tía Bernarda".

In addition, a Spanish camp of Hof (Bavaria) and the rearguard services were constituted, which included a health detachment with Spanish doctors and nurses, as well as gendarmerie services at the head of the Guardia Civil, which were distributed along the route from Spain to the Russian front.

The Blue Division's Order of Battle upon arrival at the front (based on C. Caballero's work):

250th Infantry Division known in the Wehrmacht as Infanterie Division 250 (spanische).

IN SPANISH	IN GERMAN
Plana mayor.	Stab
Regimiento de Infantería 262.	Infanterie Regiment 262 (span.)
Regimiento de Infantería 263.	Infanterie Regiment 263 (span.)
Regimiento de Infantería 269.	Infanterie Regiment 269 (span.)
Regimiento de Artillería 250.	Artillerie Regiment 250 (span.)
Batallón de Reserva Móvil.	
Grupo de Exploración 250.	Aufklärungs Abteilung (span.)
Grupo Antitanque 250.	Panzerjäger Abteilung 250 (span.)
Batallón de Zapadores 250.	Pionier Bataillon 250 (span.)
Grupo de Transmisiones 250.	Nachriten Abteilung 250 (span)
Grupo de Intendencia 250.	
Grupo de transporte 250.	Kommandeur Division Nachshub Führer 250 (span.)
Grupo de Sanidad 250.	Sänitats Abteilung 250 (span)
Compañía Veterinaria 250.	Veterinärkompanie 250 (span)
Sección de Gendarmería 250.	Feldgendarmerietrupp 250 (span.)
Estafeta Postal Militar 250.	Feldpostamt 250 (span)

Life in Grafenwöhr was spent between instruction in closed order, which was not hard given the seniority of most of the volunteers, and leisure time in the canteens, where they drank beer and sang Spanish songs and hooked up with the girls in the surrounding villages.

The issue of meals was problematic, the great difference between Spanish and German cuisine meant that they could not tolerate the greasy sausages, the enormous amount of cabbages and potatoes and especially the strange black bread. Breakfast choked them and the coffee had nothing to do with what they were used to drinking. And if that wasn't enough, the cold afternoon ranch, with canned meat, was the ultimate affront to them. Then there was the yellowish, loose German tobacco and its scarcity, as six cigarettes twice a day were totally insufficient for the heavy Hispanic smokers. The guripas very much missed the appetizing Spanish stews, from a paella to a cocido madrileño, passing through a Galician pot, a Basque marmitako or an Asturian fabada (all delicious typical Spanish meals). As a consequence of all this, Muñoz Grandes saw, on July 26, a telegram to the Minister of the Army in Madrid asking for help, since he requested the dispatch of a railway convoy with enough supplies to establish a depot in Germany so that his men could taste Spanish food at least two or three times a week.

The preparation having been completed much earlier than the Germans had planned, the 250th Division formed up on the morning of July 31 to take the Oath of Allegiance to the Führer only to fight against USSR. General Muñoz Grandes drew his sword and as he put his hand on the blade, Commander Troncoso pronounced: "Do you swear by God and by your honor as Spaniards absolute obedience to the supreme commander of the German army, Adolf Hitler, in the fight against communism and to fight as brave soldiers, ready at any moment to sacrifice your lives in fulfilment of this oath?" And the Spaniards, with their arms outstretched, shouted, "Yes, we swear." General von Cochenhausen then welcomed the 250th Division to the Wehrmacht, followed by harangues from Muñoz Grandes and General Fromm.

The next morning the units returned to combat training, astonishing the Germans with their skill and rapidity with which they dismantled their Mauser rifles, which was natural given that the vast majority of them were veterans of the civil war and those who were not had been trained, in their spare time. by the veterans. The casual attitude of the guripas, if not 100%, about the rules of uniformity made the instructors scold them, which caused tensions, since it was common not to have the clasp or top button of the jacket fastened and for the blue shirt to appear under it peeking out of her collar, as well as to wear the hat tilted and all this without noting the discomfort caused by seeing how they flirted with German girls in the surrounding villages.

The division's artillery received a total of 36 pieces of the 105/28 FH 18 Howitzer and 12 150/30 heavy howitzers. The Germans did not know that the Spaniards knew these pieces very well, having used them in the recent civil war. It was curious to see how the instructors fired with the usual Germanic rigidity and then to see the Spaniards, who seemed to swarm around the howitzer without knowing what they were doing, but who managed to fire one more shot per minute to the total astonishment of the instructors, who said that it was impossible.

For its part, the anti-tank company received the well-known Pak 37 parts. They hoped to receive all-terrain vehicles for transport, but to their surprise they were given passenger cars requisitioned in France by the Wehrmacht and it was curious to see the Peugeots, Packards and Hudsons towing the Pak 37s.

After a month's stay at Grafenwöhr, the Blue Division began embarking on trains on 21 August to leave for the front. But to the surprise of the guripas, the trains stopped in the village of Raczki, Poland, where they disembarked. Once the entire division arrived, a march on foot began to join Army Group Center under the command of Marshal von Bock, which was more than 100 km away.

There has been speculation about this German decision, although it seems that it was most likely because they considered the Spanish division poorly educated, since in those days the confidence in the Blue Division of the Wehrmacht high command was totally nil.

While this was going on, the German Liaison Detachment had been set up at Grodno under Major von Oertzen. The function of this detachment was to serve as a center of coordination and communication between the Spanish and German commands, providing translation and combat liaison services, in addition to reporting to the Führer as to the morale, combat capacity, discipline and general conduct of the 250th Division.

Von Oertzen, who constantly complained about the misconduct to the General Staff of the Blue Division, which had been installed in Treuburg, about the behaviour of the guripas in the city and reiterated the prohibition of exchanging supplies, especially tobacco, for food. He insisted that soldiers should wear their jackets buttoned up, their caps on, their belts fastened and, above all, they should salute the German officers. And it was especially insisted that fraternization with Jewish women, easily identifiable by the yellow Star of David they wore on their clothes, was absolutely forbidden.

The Komandantur was so concerned about fraternization that they authorized the Spaniards to visit the exclusive brothels of the Wehrmacht, for which they were given the appropriate condoms. In addition, rumours circulated among the guripas that they had been given anti-erotic pills and, as if that were not enough, the prohibition of fraternising with Polish women was strengthened. Totally outraged by all this, the guripas went on to retaliate and so the 10th Company of the 262nd, commanded by Captain Portolés, showed their displeasure by parading, before the German officers, wearing inflated condoms attached to the muzzles of their rifles.

These incidents, along with alarming reports of persistent Spanish intimacy with "people of the Jewish race," forced the dispatch of a liaison officer to observe and report daily. The German griddles missed the delicate problems of integrating a unit of foreign volunteers into the Wehrmacht, and even more so, the political ramifications of the Blue Division's role in the Eastern Campaign.

Before moving on to the deployment of the Spanish unit, let us recall the composition of a Regiment of the Blue Division, as well as a Company based on the work of Carlos Caballero:

Order of Battle of a Regiment of the Blue Division:

Headquarters
Command and Staff.
1st Battalion:
- 1st Rifle Company
- 2nd Rifle Company.
- 3rd Rifle Company.
- 4th Support Arms Company.

2nd Battalion:
- 5th Rifle Company
- 6th Rifle Company.
- 7th Rifle Company.
- 8th Support Arms Company.

3rd Battalion:
- 9th Rifle Company
- 10th Rifle Company.
- 11th Rifle Company.
- 12th Support Arms Company.

13th Infantry Cannon Company.
14th Anti-Tank Company.
15th Staffing Company.
Transmissions Section.
Assault Sappers Section.
Cycling section (reconnaissance).

Order of Battle of a Rifle Company:

Headquarters
Staff.
1st Section:
- 1st platoon.
- 2nd Platoon.
- 3rd Platoon.
- Mortar squad.

2nd Section:
- 1st platoon.
- 2nd Platoon.
- 3rd Platoon.
- Mortar squad.

3rd Section:
- 1st platoon.
- 2nd Platoon.
- 3rd Platoon.
- Mortar squad.

Anti-tank rifle platoon.
Battle Train.
Train of nurseries.
Baggage train.

▲ Photograph of the camp of the Blue Division soldiers marching to the Polish front.

▼ Picture of soldiers of the Spanish Volunteer Division being instructed in the handling of heavy machine guns. In the LEV both the 1st and 2nd Flags had a machine gun and mortar company. Public domain.

▲ The Spanish soldiers, although their behaviour was less severe than that of the Germans, were generally always highly appreciated by the various German units they encountered in combat. Public domain.

▲ Soldiers with a 75/36 calibre Pak 40 anti-tank gun (BVD).

▼ Divisional artillerymen inside a mortar unit (summer 1943) loading a 220 mm French Schneider heavy mortar shell (BVD).

▲ Nurses treating soldiers beneath a train (BVD).
▼ Transport of a PAK 40 75 mm anti-tank gun (BVD).

▲ Major Reinlein observes enemy positions (BVD).

Deployment

On 24 September, an order was received for the 250th Army to be transferred to Marshal Günther von Kluge's Fifth Army to be integrated into the attack on Moscow. But despite the fact that the campaign was to begin at the end of September, the Spanish division was instructed to follow a circuitous route to the starting point of the assault at Smolensk.

As they advanced across the Polish plain, the Guripas began to see the traces of the battle and this scene of a tremendous struggle left them stunned, clearly appreciating that the battle had been hard fought and paid for at a good price, for the Soviets had not surrendered, finally reaching Grodno. Once past Grodno, the division split into three groups to head for Vilnius.

On 14 September Major von Oertzen presented himself to Marshal von Bock at Borisov and there he was informed that von Kluge had refused to accept the 250th Division, saying whether it was made up of soldiers or Gypsies. As a result, the Blue Division would be transferred to the Ninth Army under General Strauss. On the other hand, Marshal von Bock ordered von Oertzen to give General Muñoz Grandes copies of all the negative reports he had exchanged with the OKH. Just two days later, Captain Günther Collatz joined the liaison detachment from the Führer's reserve. Von Ottzen's replacement had arrived unbeknownst to him.

When they finally arrived in Minsk, the Spaniards were surprised to see the impressive highway that linked this city with Moscow and along which they began to march with their flags unfurled.

The pace of progress slowed as they left Orsha behind, as splendid asphalt sections gave way to unfinished chunks of stone and gravel.

On 26 September the Division stopped for a necessary rest and recovery of strength. It was located in a swampy area, so swarms of mosquitoes preyed on the guripas and their horses. For this reason, they lit large bonfires where they could warm themselves while their intense smoke drove away the mosquitoes. In the afternoon of that day. "Radio Macuto" (the rumours within the Division) reported that the Division was going to turn around in order to return to Orsha and then turn north to head for Vitebsk, this was confirmed very soon, given that the division had just been transferred from the 9th Army of Army Group Center to the 16th Army of Army Group North. This order had been given directly by Adolf Hitler. That is why he was not going to take part in the attack on Moscow, but would assume a defensive role, which greatly disappointed the guripas.

Leningrad Front: Novgorov

The Blue Division was assigned a sector north of Novgorod, covering the bank of the Volkhov River from north of Podbereze to Chunovo, right at the point where the blown up bridge of the October Railway (from Leningrad to Moscow) was located, a sector occupied by the 126th Infantry Division commanded by General Paul Laux and which he immediately began to relieve in its positions and while some units entered in the line of fire along the Volkhov, others boarded lousy rough trains at Vitebsk, 450 km away, which would take them to Dno, where the infantry would then move onto trains running on the German gauge, while useful vehicles and horses would move along the Novgorod road.

But critical German eyes were watching the volley, the I Army Corps had sent a special team, under Captain Wessel, to observe and report on the Division and on the German Liaison Detachment. Captain Wessel reported that "the 250th Division was structured like any other similar German unit and, with few exceptions, armed in a similar manner." For the first time, General von Both had concrete information about the Spanish Division, since neither he nor his General Staff had any idea, since they did not even have information about the German liaison detachment.

On October 10, orders were suddenly cancelled to relieve the 126th Division between Podvereze and Chudovo and move south to Novgorod, where they replaced the southern units of the 126th. The Blue Division's deployment spanned from the northern tip of Lake Ilmen south of Miasmi Bor in Zmeisko.

Thus, on the night of October 12, the Spaniards of the 2nd and 3rd Battalions of the 262nd Regiment relieved two battalions of Colonel Werner von Erdmannsdorff's 30th Regiment on the island of Novgorod. To the south of the small Volkhov, in Kirillovskoe there was a monastery that the Germans had turned into a small bastion that the Soviets tried again and again to conquer without success, so Lieutenant Colonel Richter, of the 42nd Regiment, proud of his men said that they were defending it as the Alcázar of Toledo (an important siege during the Spanish Civil war) and the name Alcázar prevailed and that is why when the Pimentel Regiment arrived he found a symbol of his own civil war.

Once the division was definitively installed at the front, the Pimentel Regiment and the 250th Reconnaissance Group covered its southern sector, from Erunovo to Grigorovo; the 263rd Regiment of Vierna covered the central sector, between Grigorovo and Chechulino, and the Esparza regiment did so in the northern sector, from Chechulino to Krutik.

Volkhov River Front

The Volkhov River, which connects the lakes Ilmen (south of Leningrad) and Ladoga (east of Leningrad), became an important line separating the two sides.

The Offensive was ordered by the Führer's Headquarters, and on October 16 the Spanish artillery unleashed a heavy barrage fire to which the Russians responded without delay. Colonel Esparza received the order to send a patrol to raid through the Volkhov, leaving the place and time to his discretion and appointed Commander Roman, head of the 2nd Battalion, to carry out the order, who commissioned Lieutenant Galiana to command an assault platoon.

Shortly afterwards when he was on his way with his men to cross the river, he observed that a Soviet battalion was crossing it at that moment, so the guripas immediately went into action. Dawn revealed the corpses of 40 Russians on the Spanish shore and the remains of their boats, with 27 prisoners taken and all without a single Spanish casualty.

On the afternoon of November 19, Lieutenant Escolano crossed the Volkhov at Udarnik, passed through the minefields, and with his platoon fell upon the Soviets, who fled leaving abundant booty and 42 prisoners. He then placed his two MG 34 machine guns waiting for a planned Russian counterattack, which a few hours later was carried out by the 2nd Battalion of the 848th Rifle Regiment, which was effectively repulsed. Then it was the turn of the 3rd Battalion of the same regiment, but after a hard hand-to-hand fight they were forced to retreat. At about 11 p.m. the Russians attacked again, but without the impetus of the previous occasions. After a little more than an hour and supported by a heavy artillery attack, the Russians managed to break through the Spanish line, but Escobedo kept two platoons in reserve that attacked the Russians by surprise with all the fury of which the Spanish infantry is capable. Surprised, they hesitated and scattered into the forest. The bridgehead achieved by the 2nd Battalion of the 269th was consolidated.

On the morning of the next day, the Germans, unaware of the Spanish success, were concerned that the two bridgeheads obtained by the 126th Division were isolated, since the Wehrmacht after four days of fighting had managed to conquer a square of 20 km on each side. Setting aside the doubts and hesitations of the German command, the Spaniards began to send reinforcements across the river. Two companies of the 269th crossed under intense, but ineffective, artillery fire. They were followed by the 11th Cycling Company and the 9th of the 3rd Battalion of the 269th, as well as the 10th and 11th of the 3rd Battalion of the 263rd, as well as the 2nd Anti-Tank Company. The latter was eager to confront the Russian T-26s, which they knew well since the Spanish war, with their Pak 37s.

It was attacked in the direction of Zmeisko and the gurus of Commander Roman conquered it. The Cycling Company advancing in the direction of Sheselevo encountered a mounted reconnaissance unit of the 126th Division, thus linking the Spanish and German sides.

The following days were very hard and with frequent fighting, in which the Spaniards wasted courage, managing to occupy the towns of Sitno and Tigoda.

The 250th Reserve Battalion, as we said before better known as "La Tía Bernarda" was one of the best units of the Spanish division, because although its official name indicated that it was a depot unit, it was actually an exceptional shock unit, made up mainly of veterans of the Spanish forces in Morocco: The Legión and the Regulares. Well acquainted with Soviet weaponry, they dedicated themselves to keeping for themselves as many machine guns, automatic rifles and above all PPSH submachine guns, as well as the enormous amount of ammunition captured. That is why we can say without a doubt that it was the best armed Battalion in the Blue Division.

On October 24 the Wehrmacht mentions the Blue Division in its reports and thus the OKW says: "In defending itself against a Soviet counterattack, the Spanish division, in the northern sector of the Eastern Front, has repulsed the enemy, causing numerous casualties and taking several hundred prisoners."

On 2 November, two rifle battalions of the Russian 305th Division went into action on Niklkino. They rushed at the Spanish positions shouting "Urrah" and "Ispanskii Kaput", but the MG 34s, which the Spaniards kept from the fire to prevent them from freezing, began their rapid rattle. The Russians advance upright, waiting for the sound of their officer's whistle. None of them tried to crouch, although their comrades were falling beside them, so that if the officer was delayed or dead, they were still standing, falling one after the other. Such a sheepish attitude was totally incomprehensible to the Spaniards.

After the Soviet attack failed, at 11 a.m. it was all over, but the guripas, in their trenches, shouted to those who fled: "Another Bull," "Another Bull".

The 3rd of the 263rd had 15 killed and 50 wounded including 5 officers, but in front of its trenches lay the corpses of 221 of its attackers.

The temperature, which had been hovering around 0º, began to drop and take its toll on the Spaniards, as winter clothing did not arrive and especially the feet froze when they had to stand in the sentinel services, as they wore simple boots of fine leather. It can be said that during the winter of 1941 to 1942 only a third of Spaniards received warm boots. That is why, just as their German comrades did, before burying them they recovered from the Russian corpses their excellent boots, leather jackets, trousers and quilted jackets.

General Muñoz Grandes was ordered to extend his lines to a total active front of 60 km without weakening Novgorod, so he decided to personally make an assessment of the situation. On 16 November, he crossed the Volkhov to meet with Colonel Esparza, with whom he discussed the situation at the bridgehead and probable Russian movements. The Blue Division was to defend the narrow 18 km ledge that cut through the frozen swamps and forest, from Shevelevo to Ostenkii and Posad. It should be borne in mind that the Spaniards would replace an entire regiment with a single battalion, for which Esparza recommended the 1st of the 269th, reasoning that it had suffered few casualties and that because of the ardent Madrid Falangists who composed it they would fight as much or better than the others. Muñoz Grandes then went to Sitno to inspect the bridgehead.

In these days the guripas received the new winter underwear, but the Spanish initiative made them put it on the uniform, because in addition to serving for their mission of warming the body more, it would serve as a camouflage uniform, given its white color.

On November 11, when he passed to another destination, General Franz von Roques, who was appreciated by all the Spanish commanders, was dismissed, being replaced by General von Chappuis, who arrived full of prejudices against the Spaniards, possibly because of Major von Oertzen who figured in his General Staff. On the evening of that day the Russians with the 305th Rifle Division and part of the 3rd Armoured Division launched a strong offensive in order to conquer Otenskii, Posad and Poselok, also attacking in Russa, Dubrovka and Nikltkino. The whole front was burning!

Possad with a perimeter of 5 km had been attacked all day by endless artillery and mortar fire, which came to knock down everything that rose from the ground: trees, huts and sheds, so that only a few pillboxes and trenches were available to try to protect themselves and, as if this were not enough, ammunition was becoming scarce.

In the early hours of Thursday, the 13th, the Russians belonging to the 1004th Regiment attempted the assault on the Otenskii Monastery, but were repulsed by their defenses and taking advantage of the success a probing patrol was sent to Possad, as they were still unable to evacuate their wounded.

Possad was still under infernal artillery fire. At one point in his defensive perimeter, originally covered by a section, only a sergeant and two guripas remained, firing back-to-back in all directions. The enemy charged at them, but they, considering themselves already dead men, stood up in the trench all shouting,"Arriba España" ("Up with Spain!") and firing, some Russians fell, while the rest, thinking that they were in the way of the counter-attack, halted, and raising their arms, shouted "Niet Komunist" and surrendered. Astonished, one of the guripas led them to the rear, while the other two remained in the trench, but the first, reluctant to leave his comrades alone, pointed out to the Russians the command post and sent them there alone. He did so well that the prisoners asked Commander Vallespin to understand the plight of his men, who sent two guripas as reinforcements.

There, next to the command post, the corpses were piled up with their youthful faces of university students. They belonged to Colonel Rodrigo's 2nd Battalion, almost all of which was made up of members of the Falangist SEU. Possad had put an end to his university careers.

Colonels Rodrigo and Esparza decided to come to the aid of the garrison of Possad, but the evacuation of their wounded would have to wait until nightfall in order not to be seen by the enemy. However, Esparza advised Rodrigo, telling him that Possad and Otenskii could only be kept at too great a cost, so the most sensible thing to do was to withdraw. And it will avoid further unnecessary losses. The march of the wounded began at 4 p.m., happily managing to pass despite heavy Russian artillery fire.

The newly arrived Commander Tomás García Rebull, a veteran, presented himself to Colonel Esparza and he assigned him the command of Possad, replacing Commander Luque who had been wounded, while informing him of the deployment.

Given the situation, Muñoz Grandes decided to withdraw the well-trained units he had at the Novgorod bridgehead and replace them with transport and service personnel.

Esparza, who had moved his HQ to Otenskii, telephoned Muñoz Grandes and the latter told him that he had decided to relieve all of Possad's forces, because the men had fought well, he said, and it was time to share the glory and the danger. By relieving the seven companies that were there by only three, but… the number of soldiers remained the same!

Meanwhile, in Grigorovo, von Chappuis requested the presence of Muñoz Grandes, with whom he had a tense and stormy interview. Von Chappuis began by complaining about the catastrophic neglect of horses and motor vehicles and offered German officers and soldiers to advise and instruct the Spaniards in the care of transportation methods. Muñoz Grandes immediately rejected the offer as "incompatible with the honor of the Division," so von Chappuis did not mince words in reviewing the causes of the situation. Offended, Muñoz Grandes replied that "the Division had been supplied with poor quality horses and vehicles in Grafenwörh, which he had complained about at the time, but that he was told that the Division would be re-equipped with material captured from the Russians, who not only had not been delivered, but on the contrary, did not have abundant fodder or adequate mounts. nor did they have spare parts for their cars and motor vehicles. With his eyes blazing with his eyes, Muñoz Grandes finally told him "that the Germans seemed to regard their Division, whose only aim was to fight and die alongside their German comrades, rather than as a hindrance than as a help." Confused, von Chappuis asked how he had come to that conclusion and quickly, like a machine gun, gave him more than a dozen examples.

Surely von Chappuis would never have been spoken to like that by a subordinate general of his, but what he had in no way understood was that Muñoz Grandes commanded a Spanish expeditionary force within the Wehrmacht and that he represented the head of the Spanish state. And it was he, not von Chappuis, who had personally received instructions about his mission from the lips of Adolf Hitler himself in Rastenburg. Von Chappuis had not the slightest idea of the sensibility of the Spanish character, of the importance of the man before him or of the intricate international issues involved.

The next day von Chappuis sent a report to his superior Busch, who then passed it on to the OKH. The report concluded by recommending that the Spanish division leave the front as soon as possible. On the other hand, Captain Collatz. The head of the liaison detachment, who had been present at the interview, in turn sent a much more optimistic report, in which he revealed a considerable appreciation of Muñoz Grandes and his men.

Busch examined the reports and after reviewing them instructed von Leeb to have the division withdrawn and relieved by a German division, but von Leeb had other, more serious problems.

Muñoz Grandes would never accept the withdrawal and a diminution of the role of the Blue Division. What was at stake was not only honour, but perhaps Spanish sovereignty. The Blue Division had a dual mission: the first and most obvious was to participate in the fight against the USSR and the second, much more subtle, was to demonstrate to Hitler that the Spaniards would fight and accept any number of casualties. Operation Felix was being organized and the Führer had to convince himself that any invader would pay dearly for every inch of Spanish soil.

Muñoz Grandes faced a tough dilemma. Whatever the cost, Possad had to be maintained. The retreat was ruled out since the "doiches" would take it as weakness. But on the other hand, it pained his soul to see his men sacrificed for what was considered untenable. But Muñoz Grandes was so lucky that the Russians, beating the bastion in vain, decided to launch new units against the 126th Division of the Wehrmacht and gave Possad a break. On December 3, the battle of the Tikhvin salient began with an attack on the Spaniards at Nikltkino at two o'clock in the afternoon, the assault becoming generalized the next day, and the entire front covered by the Blue Division erupted. At 4 o'clock in the morning, with a temperature of 30 degrees below zero, the Russians attacked towards Possad and Otenskii, managing to reach the outer ring of the houses. It was only after four hours of hard hand-to-hand combat that they were repulsed. Otenskii was surrounded and the Russians continued to try to break through, while Dubrovka, Nikltkino and Tigoda began to be smashed by artillery. At a quarter past five in the morning two companies launched themselves on Shevelevo, but the Spaniards were waiting for them, since a deserter, led to Tigoda, had reported the attack, as well as that the HQs would be the targets. As soon as the Russians approached, they were greeted by a hail of hand grenades and heavy fire that tore them apart. A detachment proceeded to examine the corpses, discovering, under their white garments, uniforms of all arms and services. Among them were former officers, pilots and even health workers. It was a punishment unit sent to life and death. Russian losses that day amounted to 550 dead at the cost of the lives of 130 Spaniards, too many for the decimated Spanish battalions.

Von Chappuis was concerned about the potential decrease in his units. That night he discussed the matter with his boss von Busch, telling him that the 126th was at its limit and that the vital Chudovo crossing point was in danger. The Spaniards had the same problem, but theirs was especially acute because of the 110 km length of their front. Chudovo was in 126th while 250th covered Novgorod.

"I don't think the Spaniards will be able to hold on to Novgorod in the face of a strong Russian attack," von Chappuis continued. Busch replied: "The head of the Blue Division has told me that especially on the Novgorod front you will be able to hold your positions." With this resounding comment he made it very clear that he raised Muñoz Grandes and trusted him, because, although worried about the Spaniards, he did not allow himself to be carried away by panic. Von Chappuis had been led to adopt a hasty opinion, and now he was paying for it. He had lost the confidence of his army chief, while one of his subordinates was on his way to winning it. But Muñoz Grandes had to prove that his men could hold out. Possad and Otenskii were somewhat under attack by the 305th Fusiliers. The weather changed suddenly and an incredible cold of 35º below zero assailed the Spaniards. The Russians attacked again with reserves brought from Poselok, while their planes and guns pounded the Spanish positions at Possad. The attack began at 8:35 a.m., with drunken riflemen from the 1002nd and 1004th regiments converging on all sides of Possad, supported by light tanks from the 3rd battalion of the 5th Armoured Division. They ran over the listening posts and when they rushed into the most advanced sniper pits, they finished off the wounded guripas with ice picks and trench shovels, but that was the limit of their advance.

At last, von Chappuis proposed a retreat, but this had been postponed by the commander of Army Group North (von Busch) pending the construction of defensive positions, but von Chappuis had not yet given the order to do so. Secretly, without informing his superior, Muñoz Grandes prepared to evacuate his men. This was a serious breach of authority, and Muñoz Grandes knew it.

On the night of December 6, he sent his deputy, Rodrigo, to Shevelevo with verbal orders for Esparza indicating that the retreat had been fixed in principle for the night of December 7-8. And above all, the retreat had to be done in perfect order and with the minimum number of casualties. Thus, at 4:30 p.m. on the night of the 7th, Muñoz Grandes ordered the retreat to begin at 9 p.m.

Deeply concerned and totally ignorant of what was going on under his very nose, von Chappuis telephoned von Busch at 7 p.m. recommending that the 250th Division withdraw through the Volkhov, to which the Volkhov agreed, as he had already given orders in the morning to evacuate Tikvin. The order to withdraw was given at 10 p.m. 14 p.m., when the garrison of Possad had already passed Otenskii and the men of the Monastery were moving west in perfect order. The battalions set fire to the villages before retreating across the icy river. The last truck, which left Sitno, was carrying the crosses from the cemetery where the remains of the fallen Spaniards rested.

"Nail yourselves to the ground", "Not one step back" repeated Muñoz Grandes. It was clear what he meant, the new line would be maintained at all costs.

Von Chappuis, as usual, doubted that he would hold out. In his opinion, the Spanish general seemed more concerned with getting his men out (who had broken contact with the Russians without suffering a single casualty) than with saving supplies and artillery. In Itenskii the provisions had been given to the guripas, who freely stocked up on chocolate and cognac, and instead of loading the trucks with the remaining rations, the Spaniards used them to transport their wounded. When the head of the Army Corps reproached Muñoz Grandes for this, he was singularly unperturbed. Or, as we Spaniards like to say: "He didn't pay any fucking attention to him".

▲ Divisionary photograph at the outdoor radio station (BVD).

▼ Cathedral of St. Sophia in Novgorod. Spanish soldiers of the Blue Division removed the large main cross and transferred it to Spain, where it remained until November 2004 (BVD).

▲ Soldiers of the Blue Division having fun in the snowy Soviet landscape (BVD).

▼ The Blue Division on its way to the Eastern Front. Volunteers share sausages in a moment of conviviality (BVD).

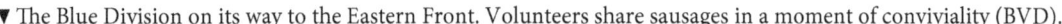

▲ General Wilhelm Ritter von Leeb delivers a speech, behind him General Agustín Muñoz Grandes (BVD).

▼ A sentinel on the walls of the Novgorod Kremlin (BVD).

▲ The military attaché in Berlin, Lieutenant Colonel Moyano, visits the front (BVD).

▲ Spanish cemetery, possibly Sluzk. Partial view, with a cross commemorating the fallen in the battles of Posselok. Cross with the national flag in force at the time, at half-mast (BVD).

▲ Gun on ruins (BVD).

▼ Portrait of a group of divisionaries next to a German counter-tank (BVD).

▲ Three soldiers handle a gun (BVD).

▼ Each convalescent in the Blue Division was given a parcel containing various items, including a portrait of the Führer (BVD).

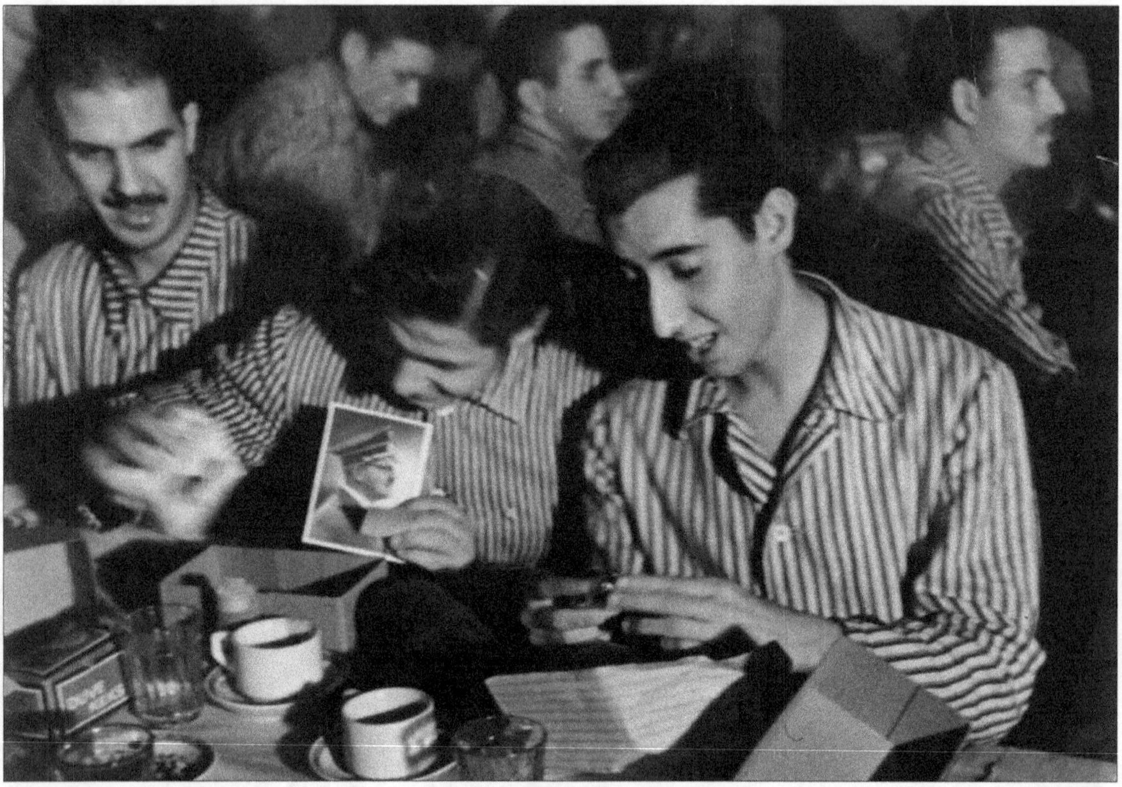

▲ Decoration Ceremony (BVD).

▼ Blue Division soldier with rifle and steel helmet guarding a wooden bridge (BVD).

▲ Portrait of two soldiers of the Division at the entrance to a shelter (BVD).

▲ Senior Spanish and German military commanders, each wearing their own uniform (BVD).
▼ High military and Spanish commanders greet a nurse (BVD).

▲ Decorated divisionary Juan Chicharro Lamamie de Clairac in his winter uniform (BVD).

▲ Photograph of post office manager receiving mail (BVD).

▲ General Moscardó greets the brave NCOs decorated with the Iron Cross for their heroism in the fighting in December 1941. Photo shows brave Luis Nieto receiving the decoration (BVD).

▼ Corporals Agustín Barrios and Herminio González García pose for the camera. Note the unofficial DA coat of arms of the corporal on the left in the photo (BVD).

▲ General Emilio Esteban Infantes in conversation with a German comrade (BVD).

On December 18, Hitler succumbed to the inevitable and announced that due to the premature and harsh winter weather, major offensives were paralyzed and he went on the defensive.

It became increasingly apparent that only the Volkhov would provide a winter defensive line. The Spaniards were there, and von Busch had gratefully found that the 250th Division could hold out. Muñoz Grandes reorganized his meager forces to gain some depth in the defense, which had only ten days to rest, while the 126th and the 23rd Army Corps were being harassed behind their lines by the Russian partisans, who were wreaking havoc on their supply columns and breaking their communications.

On 20 December, the 126th and the rest of the German units were ordered to retreat and cross the Volkhov river.

On December 25, the Russians began Christmas by launching an attack on Udarnik, whose garrison, formed by the 7th and 8th Companies of the 269th and the 5th Anti-Tank Section, managed to repel under the command of Commander Roman.

At 2:30 a.m., Captain Temprano informed Colonel Esparza from Lobkovo that from the north, in the direction of the new "Intermedia" position (mid-way position), an intense fire was heard and that he did not know what was happening because he had not had time to lay a telephone line.

In the "Intermedia", Ensign Rubio Moscoso, who had commanded it since the day before, only a few sniper pits had been dug. There was no news until a wounded and staggering sergeant, sent by the Ensign, arrived to report that they were under heavy attack and had come out with two soldiers, but that on reaching the Lobkovo-Udarnik road, 300 yards to the rear, they ran into a long Soviet column heading north. in the direction of Urdaniz. A clearing in the column gave them the opportunity, they came out of the forest and broke through the enemy formation, being spotted and attacked, the Sergeant was wounded, but still managed to escape, but his comrades fell there.

At minus 36° a platoon went out for reconnaissance, heading north, in the direction of the Germans of the 126th at Plostishno and Lieutenant Ochoa's section southward, to Lockovo. The lieutenant, known to his men as "El Alcalde" (for he had resigned as mayor of Ceuta to enlist in the Blue Division) led his thirty-two men along the path of the minefield until they reached the Udarnik-Lobkovo road. It was 3:30 a.m. and there were eight hours of darkness left.

Little was seen and nothing could be heard, as the rustle of the trees and the strong wind with snow limited visibility to a few meters. And so, suddenly, the two columns struck each other head-on, to each other's surprise, all throwing themselves into the ditches and opening fire. Five guripas fell and Ochoa was hit. Dragging their wounded, the battered section managed to reach Udarnik.

Commander Román called Colonel Esparza and reported: "The situation is serious, my Colonel. Lieutenant Eight has a serious wound in the chest, and we have lost fifteen out of thirty-two men. The enemy seems to be very numerous."

Esparza replied to Román that he had alerted Lieutenant Petenghi with his assault section and Vallespín in Miasnoi Bor. They would go by truck south to Udarnik, but unfortunately it would be several hours before they arrived.

The Colonel also indicated that Garcia Rebull was on his way north, from Vitka to Lobkovo and that with the available reinforcements they would attack Udarnik down and up from Lobkovo, enveloping the Russians from the Intermediate position. Román hung up and asked for a volunteer to check what was happening in the Intermediate position, and the guru Mariano Ferrer showed up, who immediately went there.

He then ordered a retreat to the outer posts, and the Russians followed, occupying the southernmost huts, but not attacking, as they contented themselves with shrapneling the houses and shelling the town with mortars. Colonel Esparza, knowing that there was a German dump in Miasnoi Bor, called his boss on the phone, explained the situation and gave him the coordinates of the map, but the Germans refused to give their support.

At 6:30 a.m., Commander Román called Colonel Esparza: "We are surrounded by a battalion, my Colonel. The thirty men I have left are barricaded in the chapel and in a few nearby huts. I'm going to fight back."

"I think I should wait," replied Esparza, "for Villaspin and Petenghi to arrive, and then we'll catch them between two fires."

Pushing the Pak 37, the anti-tank guns came out of the chapel and their small cannon barked again while the guripas advanced with a clean blast. The wounded who were still walking were shooting and stumbling. The cannon fired into the window of an isba (typical Russian peasant home) 200 meters away and the guripas took it by assault while two other guripas who had been captured shortly before, came out shouting "Arriba España!" and taking rifles, they joined the assault. By 7:30 a.m. Urdanik was once again in Spanish hands. Petenghi showed up three minutes later and Vallespín at 9 a.m. The 126th Division had in the meantime repulsed the Russian attack on Ploshtino and, realizing that the main Soviet assault had taken place in the Spanish sector, immediately sent four companies to Urdanik to help the Spaniards, but the Russians had already put their feet on the ground by the time they arrived.

Roman then led the column south, past rows of Russian corpses. Garcia Rebull was simultaneously advancing northward from Lobkovo. A patrol was advancing, making way for Roman's relief column. Helmets, weapons, corpses and equipment were strewn across the road and forests. The icy body of a Spanish corporal appeared at the rendezvous point of the previous night, and in front of him was the hill of the "Intermedia" position. The scouts set out in search of the road, discovering between the lines the soldier Mariano Ferrer, who was still alive trying to crawl towards them. When they picked him up, they found that he had been injured three times and that all his fingers were frozen and there was no choice but to amputate them. Climbing the slope toward the "Intermedia" position, the scouts passed among dozens of Russian corpses. The patrol crested the hill. Silence. Then there were cries of rage and anguish. The political commissars had done their homework. The Spaniards had been pinned to the ground with ice picks and the wounded finished off. A primitive roar of anguish swept through the Spanish ranks. While Román and García Rebull's troops pursued the Russians, those of Petenghi's assault section, responding furiously, hunted the Soviets in the woods. Smelling on the open ice of the Volkhov, the soldiers of the 1002nd and 1004th were uncetemoniously mowed. The situation was restored by noon. No prisoners were taken.

The Commissars gathered their men for a new assault. At 2 p.m., the remnants of three battalions, about two companies, left Russa through the ice and attacked the old chapel. Lieutenant Escobedo was wounded at the first volley. Overwhelming the section, the Russians again began their dreadful task, but before they could finish they arrived at forced marches from Lobkovo with two companies of the 1st of the 269th. Within ten minutes, the Russians had been dislodged from the hill and pushed back into the ice. None survived. According to the body count, the Russians lost in action amounted to 1,080 dead, with no prisoners; Spanish casualties were 3 officers killed and 4 wounded, and to 32 non-commissioned officers and soldiers killed and 61 wounded, all of the 269th Regiment.

Muñoz Grandes felt the rage and fury that now dominated his men. To channel his emotions, to calm them down, and to show that he shared their pain, he issued the following proclamation:

"The action that began on the 24th ended yesterday the 27th, with the maximum effort of the enemy. With forces vastly superior to ours, he tried to break through our lines. I am fully satisfied with you and wish to pay tribute of gratitude to those brave men of the Middle Position who carried out the order: "It is impossible to retreat, you must resist as if you were nailed to the ground." None of them retreated. During the brief time they occupied the position, the Russian barbarians pinned our dead and wounded to the ground with spikes. The order was carried out to the letter.... For once, red bestiality has served to make the bravery of our soldiers more sublime. I'm so proud to be Spanish!".

Muñoz Grandes

The Ilmen Lake achievement

On January 7, 1942, all hell broke loose in the southern sector of the 16th Army. The Soviets broke the line of the Lovat River and advanced 50 km to the outskirts of Staraia Russa, the main supply center of the 10th and 2nd Army Corps. Four Soviet mobile armies converged on six German armies in a static defense line.

In this winter war, without a front line, German units were isolated and surrounded. One of them, a small one, of the 290th Division, defended Vivad, at the mouth of the Lovat River. Captain Prölh commanded his small garrison, which was soon joined by the remnants of the overflowing posts. Struggling to survive, X Corps could not detach itself from any unit to come to someone's aid. The plea for help went to the 16th Army. Von Busch was throwing everything he could into battle: police forces, Latvians, Russian local guards. He looked for some way out and, remembering the Spanish reconnaissance on the ice of Lake Ilmen, ordered von

Chappuis to dispatch a Spanish unit to come to help and relief the German garrison in Vsvad.

Faced with the ballot that the Germans gave them, Muñoz Grandes did not hesitate to accept it, despite not having any reserves available. However, it was decided that it would be the Company of Skiers, based in Samokritzha under the command of Captain Ordás, and in which two hundred guripas were formed.

The thermometer read 32° below zero, when on Saturday, January 10, 1942, the 205 men of the company formed up in their white winter clothes before their Captain. The General had sent his adjutant, Lieutenant Commander Mora Figueroa, to wish them good luck at their departure point at Spaso-Piskopets. "You are going to liberate a battalion of German comrades," he said. "Go ahead," cried Ordás, with all the strength of his lungs, and he began to walk. Beside him walked a stout, middle-aged figure, whose shadow almost absorbed that of the little Captain. Ordás cast a confident glance at his partner, Sergeant Willi Klein, a German interpreter attached by the Liaison Detachment to the Ski Company. They had not had time to make friends, but Klein had lived in Spain, as a merchant in Bilbao, before the civil war and was a prisoner of the Reds until he was freed by the Nationalists. Klein had a great deal of respect for Ordás, whose bearing had earned him the nickname "The Prussian" by his men.

The company ploughed on, carrying provisions and equipment on the sleds. The sleighs and horses had been requisitioned, but the peasants, fearful that they would not be returned, offered themselves as drivers. A total of 70 muzhiks (Russian civilians) accompanied the Spanish relief force.

A few hours into the march, Ordás called Radio Varela to report the advance to Headquarters, but the radio's generator had frozen. Without hesitation, Ordás ordered Valera to turn for another. "You know the way," he said calmly. "Catch up with us as soon as you can."

The cold was painful, the sun rose, but it still didn't give warmth. Ordás followed the course of the compass around deep crevasses and great ice shelves, raised by the waves on the surface of the lake. Meanwhile, Varela and his team began their return trying to accomplish their mission.

Finally, Varela arrived and introduced himself to his captain in accordance with the regulations, just as the "Prussian" liked it.

Following the initiation of contact with the Division, the following communications were received:

1 January, 9:30 p.m. Muñoz Grandes to Ordás: "The garrison of Vsvad is bravely holding on… It is absolutely necessary to help them. The honour of Spain and the spirit of fraternity of our people demand it."

11 January, 2 h. Muñoz Grandes to Ordás: "You are the pride of our race, trust in God and attack as Spaniards."

The march continued, at minus 53°, and after what seemed like a never-ending march, as the planned eight hours had turned into twenty-two, the Skiers' Company reached the southern shore of Lake Ilmen near Istrika. Two sentinels of the 81st Division watched nervously as a column of soldiers approached their post. One of them made an effort to see something and said to his companion, "There are the reds." A sergeant and several soldiers were immediately deployed. Seeing the shadows in the morning light, the sergeant shouted, "Stoj!" "A voice answered, 'German?' And again: German?" "I'm sorry, Sergeant," one of his men shouted. Don't throw away, they're Spanish." Then a voice was heard in German: "Don't shoot. We are comrades of the Spanish Blue Division. I'm Sergeant Klein, interpreter," and Klein ran to his companions so there would be no mistake.

The Spaniards were led to what seemed to them to be a palace: a small wooden hut with a stove. And even hot tea! Then Ordás and his men knew that Vsvad was still holding out and that they would be under the temporary command of the 81st Division, deployed on the shore of Lake Ilmen. The Ski Company was a welcome reinforcement, even if it was weak. Ordás ordered the evacuation of one hundred and two of his men due to frostbite, eighteen of them with double amputations.

Safely on the southern shore of the lake, but not in Vivad, Ordás got in touch with Muñoz Grandes, whose General Staff kept a record of the messages exchanged by radio:

11 January 10.10 h. Ordás to Muñoz Grandes
After crossing the ice shelf and crossing crevasses, knee-deep in water, we arrived in Ustrika.

10.30 a.m. Muñoz Grandes to Ordás
I know about your efforts during the march…… the garrison of Vsvad still resists. You must help her at all costs, even if you freeze in the lake. You must go on, alone, if necessary, until death. You have to reach Vsvad and die with them. On behalf of the homeland, thank you. Do not lose heart, I trust you.

17 January 22 h. Ordás to Muñoz Grandes
The enemy counterattacked with two battalions, with anti-tank guns and six medium tanks, which quickly overwhelmed the Spanish vanguard. The encircled detachment defended itself heroically… Of the 36 Spaniards in La Vanguardia (Spanish newspaper), 14 died. The rest broke through the siege and joined the company, We are digging in…… And we will resist the next major attack. At 9 p.m. we received the order to establish an outpost at Maloe Utchno.

19 January 13.30 h. Ordás to Muñoz Grandes
At 7:30 a.m. today the enemy launched a mass attack on Maloe Utchno, suppressing the garrison of 25 Spaniards and 19 Germans. The attack was supported by tanks. The Company deployed and managed to rescue five wounded Spaniards and two Germans. The great concentration of the enemy prevented us from reconquering the position. The garrison did not capitulate. They died with guns in their hands. We observed a large enemy mass in the direction of Maloe Utchno. We look forward to the attack. We will know how to die like Spaniards.
11 p.m. Muñoz Grandes to Ordás
You speak as only heroes would. This is the only way to build an empire. Value. Your conduct is the pride of this brave Division. In spite of everything, you will win. There is a God and He will grant you victory, because you are the bravest sons and daughters of Spain. A hug that won't be the last.

21 January 14.30 h. Ordás to Muñoz Grandes
Last night we were bombed three times by Russian planes. In the evening, large masses of the enemy advanced against our positions. A number of volunteers have gone out to set fire to enemy tanks. The penetrating movement of the attack has been contained and the enemy retreats. God exists.
4 p.m. The Chief of the 81st Division congratulates us and awards decorations.
9.45 a.m. Ordás to Muñoz Grandes
A detachment left this morning from Maloe Utchno for Vsvad. The garrison of Vsvad, which made a sortie last night, embraced our men over the frozen lake seven kilometers east of Uzhin. Your orders have been carried out in full.
11 hours Ordás to Muñoz Grandes
Our lake strength has returned. Most have frostbite.

25 January 1.40 h. Muñoz Grandes to Ordás
Tell me how many brave people are left.
6:45 p.m. Ordás to Muñoz Grandes
There were twelve of us left.

The feat of the Ski Company and its efforts to rescue Vsvad is among the heroic episodes recorded on either side in World War II. Alone, these men fought and died, earning an immortal place in history.
In contrast to the critical comments about the Spaniards in the War Diary of the 28th Army Corps, which even went so far as to stop extolling the Company of Skiers, the Liaison Detachment rightly bursts with pride. General Schopper addressed a personal message of summons to his comrade in Grigorovo and awarded 23 Iron Crosses. General Francisco Franco sent a special message in which Ordás was awarded his second Military Medal and also the collective Military Medal to the Company of Skiers. Muñoz Grandes, proud of his men, sent a large package of documentation to report the feat to Adolf Hitler, who read it in Rastenburg.
January 15 was a black day for Army Group North, as the desire to reconquer Temerest by joint Spanish-German forces confirmed that the Russians were very firm in their bridgehead, as they had opened a gap of 6 km between the 126th and 125th divisions. Muñoz Grandes received a report in which his Chief of Information

told him that the Blue Division should not expect a frontal attack, since the Soviet commissars had been telling their men that the Spaniards had punished the 305th Rifle Division so much that they preferred to look for a weaker enemy. But there was one fact well known to all, which was that the Russian infantry was not particularly disposed to engage in hand-to-hand combat with the Spaniards. But General Franco was not so sure, because his information service revealed the German disaster in all fronts.

Consequently, Franco ordered his ambassador in Berlin, Count of Mayalde, to put pressure on the Germans to withdraw the Division from the front, but the Germans did not want to withdraw it from the front, simply because they had nothing to replace it with, so they continued to insist that the situation on the front line was not serious and that the Blue Division had a Reserve Battalion. At the beginning of January, Krappe informed General Asensio, Chief of the Spanish Central General Staff, that the battalion was in Hof and at the end of this month the OKW said that it was at the front with the division, but in all this time, Asensio had not let it be known that the 250th Reserve Battalion had been virtually annihilated in the Muravevskiia barracks in October.

In Spain, General Asensio was faced with the problem of a dwindling pool of volunteers. Returning veterans spoke of the rigors of the cold and the hard fight against an outnumbered enemy. In addition, there were complaints about the attitude of superiority of some Germans in their dealings with the Spaniards and also about the pensions for the widows and war maimed, which were slow in coming.

In order to restore the Blue Division to its full strength, a relay rotation was initiated, from April to October 1941 in two phases. In the first mixed battalions of 300 to 400 men would be sent, given ten days, and in the second marching battalions of 900 to 1,000 men. Thus, the first relief expedition arrived in Novgorod on March 26, 1942, and the 7th Marching Battalion on April 12, 1942.

All the expeditions followed the same routine: medical examination, change of uniform, handing over of personal equipment and light weapons, oath of allegiance to the Führer, and embarkation to the front. Normally each expedition was ready every week to leave Auberbach, but the 7th Battalion had to wait three weeks because the German quartermaster did not have uniforms to equip it, but finally on May 5 it arrived in Novgorod, where the distribution of its men immediately began. Colonel Sagrado would relieve Pimentel in command of the 261'2nd and he would take charge of the 1st Return Battalion, which on May 11 would board the trains that would take him back home in Grigorovo.

On May 30, Lindemann squeezed the ends of the Volkhov pocket ready to strangle the 2nd Shock Army, as he was convinced that General Vlasov was not going to retreat, but would wait for the thaw to renew the attack to the west. Vlasov, like Stalin, was desperate, for Leningrad was at the limit of its endurance and the icy road that bound it was about to crack.

On 30 May, with support from Ju-87 Stukas, the Germans attacked and within 24 hours Vlasov was again encircled. This necessitated a further transfer of Spanish troops to the north.

For this reason, Colonel Salazar, the new Chief of Staff of the Blue Division, deployed the 250th Reconnaissance Battalion and the Anti-Tank Group to Dolgovo and there they were joined by the 2nd Motorized Infantry Brigade of the Waffen SS in order to create an Army Corps reserve. Likewise, the 3rd Battalion of the 262nd, under the command of Commander Cuesta, withdrew from the front line and remained in reserve at Tiutisy for immediate intervention if the Russians began to break in.

The Russians revolted in vain against the encirclement despite their attempted attacks with T-34 tanks, heavy artillery, aviation and infantry. As the intensity of the Soviet attacks gradually increased, the Wehrmacht's ring softened and units of the 3rd Shock Army began to leak out. On 12 June, the Cuesta Group, consisting of the 250th Reconnaissance Battalion and the Anti-Tank Group, departed from Dolgovo and entered the line at Bol Zamoshe.

Meretskov and Vlasov began a last-ditch effort at 11:30 a.m. on Tuesday, June 23. The 2nd Army had gone east and the 59th west. At dawn the next day they managed to open a breach and the soldiers of the 2nd began to pass through it. But their flanks did not hold and the gap closed again at noon.

Vlasov gave the order to every man for himself, and the organized resistance collapsed. The battle of the Volkhov pocket was over.

About 16,000 Russians managed to escape, but another 14,000 remained inside the pocket. The Skier Company and the 1st of the 263rd were sent north to join the Wehrmacht's 58th Division, while Cuesta's Group continued the cleanup.

On June 28, Radio Berlin broadcast the German victory and General Lindemann addressed a special harangue to the men of the 18th Army, whose ranks included men from the Wehrmacht, Waffen SS, Dutch, Flemish and Spanish.

The Spaniards had been on the front line from the start. Clinging to Novgorod while the Russians broke through the lines of the Lovat and Volkhov, the Blue Division was the solid hinge of the XXVIII Army Corps. Spanish units were loaned to other divisions as the Germans struggled to recover. For some time, the winter offensive threatened to engulf the guripas. There were then weeks of anguish in Madrid and Grigorovo. Muñoz Grandes sent men from the support services to the fighting ranks while the German and Spanish governments discussed the issue of reinforcements. Muñoz Grandes' war was waged on three fronts: on the Volkhov, in Madrid and in Rastenburg. For this he was admired by Franco and then relieved, sending General Emilio Estaban Infantes to replace him and whose arrival in Berlin took place on June 14, 1942.

However, although General Esteban Infantes arrived in Hof on the 16th, changed his uniform for German and swore an oath to the Führer and was informed that on the 19th he would leave Berlin for the front, suddenly everything was put on hold, since Adolf Hitler did not agree at all with the handover.

Admiral Canaris was sent to Madrid, where on June 22 he was received by Franco, to whom, without revealing the Führer's wish, he simply asked for his name to be sent to the Army.

On July 11, Hitler received Muñoz Grandes in Rastenburg and in the course of the long conversation they had, Muñoz Grandes asked him if he could move the Division to a more active front, to which he agreed despite knowing that Army Group North was against it, as he did not want to lose the 250th Division.

Shortly after his return to the front, "Radio Macuto" broadcast the Division's imminent transfer from the Volkhov to the Neva. By then many of the veterans had already returned to Spain. On June 21, Colonel Rodrigo was promoted to Brigadier General and relieved. Commander Román also returned to Spain and left Captain Bonet in charge of the 2nd Battalion of the 269th which was an honor, for the battalion had a history of bravery and endurance unequalled in the entire Division. So much so that the official Soviet history of the Great Patriotic War recognizes the 2nd Battalion of the 269th Regiment as the best unit of the Blue Division.

July began with a series of beatings to the west. Forces of the three regiments went into the thicket and the swamps in order to chase in their flight and defeat the remnants of the 2nd Shock Army. Utterly demoralized and starving, the Russians willingly surrendered, and only a few managed to escape and come into contact with the partisans in the forests of the West.

To the north, the 250th Reconnaissance Division, continuing to collaborate with the Wehrmacht's 50th Division in the collection of prisoners, managed to capture more than 7,000 officers and soldiers, including the intelligence and health chiefs of the 2nd Shock, as well as 44 cannons, a large amount of light weapons and numerous materiel.

On July 12, General Vlasov was captured by two officers of the XXVIII Army Corps.

On July 25, the Spaniards undertook a trial-and-error action. Three German-manned assault boats departed loaded with guripas, and as they glided silently down the Volkhov and were halfway there, a guripa who was standing in the headboat began to sing, at the top of his lungs, the "Cara al sol". The Germans trembled at such a breach of safety regulations and wondered if they would come back alive after an action with such reckless people.

After landfall, the guripas jumped ashore and slid inland. Serving as the codename "Santiago", the three divisional groups regrouped near the road, not seeing a soul there, and consequently not a shot was fired, as the Russians had retreated to their second line.

On the 29th the Russians responded with a raid against the Monastery of Iurevo, which was garrisoned by the 1st Section of the 2nd Company of the Anti-Tank Group, under the command of Captain Oroquieta, which failed in the face of the harsh Spanish reaction. Two days later some three hundred Russians left Temerets, after a hard artillery softening in the Zapole sector, commanded by Lieutenant Colonel Bolumburu, second in command of the 263rd. The confrontation was decided in hand-to-hand combat, managing to repel them to open ground, where in broad daylight they were decimated by machine gun and mortar fire, leaving more than a hundred dead on the ground, in exchange for 19 dead and 38 wounded Spaniards.

Before dawn on July 31, the Soviet army began one of its attempts to break north from Temerets, launching itself against the Robles Group, 2nd commander of the 262nd, who enjoyed the curious distinction of having under his command a Dutch mortar company of the Nederland Regiment of the Waffen SS. as well as a later one, on August 3, they were repulsed, causing heavy casualties to the Russians.

The battle of Krasny Bor

On 11 August, the 250th Reconnaissance and the 3rd of the 262nd began the transfer of the Blue Division aboard trains. Exhausted but glad at the prospect of embarking on a great undertaking, they sang as they rolled northwest on the Novgorod-Leningrad railway line toward Susanino. Next to Susanino was Viritsa, the city designated as the base of the HQ of the Blue Division.

As the units arrived, the Battle Groups were disbanded back to their primitive regiments, and the 250th Reconnaissance began to prepare rapidly for an assault on Leningrad.

Meanwhile, General Esteban Infantes, who continued to be bored in Berlin, insisted on marching to the front, but the OKW continued to refuse him. For this reason, he wrote a letter to Muñoz Grandes asking for his mediation and the latter, on July 21, asked for authorization for Esteban Infantes to appear in Grigorovo as 2nd Chief of the Blue Division and Chief of his Infantry, but the OKH refused to do so. But Muñoz Grandes was willing to receive him into the Division and, if necessary, present him to the Germans as a fait accompli. Therefore, on August 18, Marshal von Kürchler officially learned that Esteban Infantes was on his way and that he would land in Pskov in the morning, since he had boarded the Junkers Ju-52 of the Spanish liaison that had just entered service shortly before, so he immediately consulted with the OKW, Marshal Keitel answering that Esteban Infantes had left Berlin without Hitler's permission and that he would not be allowed to replace Hitler. Muñoz Grandes was not the 3rd 2nd Chief of the 250th Division, although he could assume command of the Infantry.

General Hansen presented himself at the HQ of Vytritza, because although the Spaniards still belonged to the 50th Army Corps, they were soon going to become dependent on the 54th and Hansen wanted to get to know them now.

According to the plan of attack, the 250th Division was to leave Pushkin, along with the 28th Light and 132nd Wehrmacht, directly for Leningrad and once they reached the outskirts, the Blue Division was to extend and protect the flanks of the two German Divisions when they turned eastwards. But Meretskov attacked on August 27 and General Wodring's 26th Army Corps was subjected to a very heavy artillery and rocket attack of more than two hours followed by waves of infantry that flooded and broke their lines, managing to open a gap of eight kilometers. The Russians advanced for two days, right until the 12th Panzer Division and the 170th Panzer Division of the 30th Army Corps arrived. Meretskov's momentum first slowed and then stalled. The guripas, as usual, immediately learned, thanks to "Radio Macuto", what was happening in the Ladoga.

Von Küchler put the Blue Division on alert and on 31 August sent it north to Pushkin. Muñoz Grandes would have his men as an immediate reserve behind the 121st Division, as a new Russian attack was expected, either from Pushkin or from Kolpino.

Il 1° settembre arrivò l'ordine di iniziare la marcia al tramonto. Alle 21.30 il 1° e il 3° battaglione del 269° lasciarono Vytritza per Krasnogvardeiisk (Gatchina), la prima città russa che gli spagnoli videro indenne, senza subire le devastazioni della guerra. I *Guripas* iniziarono a cantare al passaggio della stazione di Viarlevo, città che mesi dopo, per gioco di parole, iniziarono a chiamare "Relay Village". Il 3 settembre tutte le unità, ad eccezione dell'artiglieria, avevano raggiunto Pushkin.

On the 1st of September came the order to set out at dusk. For this reason, at 9:30 p.m., the 1st and 3rd Battalions of the 269th left Vytritza for Krasnogvardeiisk (Gatchina), the first Russian city that the Spaniards saw unscathed, without suffering the ravages of war. The guripas began to sing as they passed by the Viarlevo station, a town that months later and making a play on words they began to call "Villa Relevo" (Villa Relief). By September 3 all units, with the exception of artillery, had reached Pushkin.

On the night of 5 September, General Hansen ordered the front of the Blue Division to be extended to the right and the 2nd Regiment of the SS Division "Polizei" to withdraw in front of Kolpino. For their part, the Spaniards would cross the Izhora River, cross the Leningrad-Moscow highway and fall on the embankment of the October Railway. These movements, forced by the punishment suffered by the SS "Polizei" in the Tosna, transferred to the Blue Division a sector that was eccentric to its main deployment and supply routes and that was only directly accessible by a log road. It could be reached more easily by crossing the Izhora and making a detour to the south through the forests of Sablino. Once in this locality, there was access by the road that led past the town of Krasny Bor, located between the road and the railway.

Muñoz Grandes, considering that this change would be temporary, decided to maintain his center of gravity as originally planned, between Aleksandrovka and the Izhora River. Villalba and the 263º are on the left flank; Rubio and the 269th in the center and Sagrado with the 262nd on the right flank. As for the additional and separate sector, he decided to garrison it with a force assembled for the occasion: the Robles Group, under the command of the Lieutenant Colonel of the same name and head of the 2nd Battalion of the 262nd. As usual, the Spaniards created their own reserves, having two units at the front and one in the rear. The anti-tank guns were scattered throughout the sectors. Finally, Muñoz Grandes' HQ turned its attention to Prokovskaia.

The Blue Division was facing part of the Soviet 42nd and 55th Armies. The first of these defended the area from the Gulf of Finland to Pushkin and the 55th covered ground from Pushkin to the mouth of the Tosna. Russian morale was very low and desertions were on the rise. The 72nd Division was a prison unit whose soldiers had been taken from forced labor camps in Liberia. Three strong artillery concentrations defended the southern approaches to Leningrad and the Spaniards were within range of two of them, Pulkovo and Kolpino. Around Pulkovo there were thirteen batteries and no less than forty in the Kolpino ring. In addition, the long-range guns of the Baltic Fleet were added to thirty railway batteries in Leningrad itself.

For its part, the Spanish artillery had nine batteries of medium howitzers, three heavy howitzers, plus a battery of 155 mm Schneider howitzers. Of those captured by the Germans in France and another of 220 mm mortars of the same origin. In addition, each of the Regiments had an accompanying company with five howitzers of 75 mm and two of 50 mm.

The Russians soon discovered that they had the Spaniards in front of them and quickly their propaganda loudspeakers replaced the German songs with nothing less than "Ramona" and decided to test them in the process. Thus, at about ten o'clock on the night of September 13, a hail of mortar shells reached the 1st of the 262nd and as they lengthened their shot a mass of Russians emerged from the darkness, but caught by a heavy crossfire before they managed to cross the barbed wire, they scattered and retreated, leaving behind dead and wounded. At the same time two more companies fell on the 3rd of the 262nd at Krasny Bor. The Robles Group only had light barbed wire and mines. The Reds rushed upon the sentinels and trenches of the 9th and 10th Companies. A hundred of them began to make their way through the labyrinth of the 9th position and as many others did the same in the net of the 10th. The Soviets, as usual, stopped to plunder, but Captains Pardo and Portoles at the head of their companies advanced through the dark tunnels and began to flash in the night the hand bombs, bayonets and trench shovels. Pardo was wounded and refused to be evacuated and Portolés, pistol in hand, advanced unstoppable. Suddenly it was all over, the Russian soldiers were fleeing in a stampede, but the 3rd artillery opened fire from the Ishora and caught them in open ground making a carnage. Portolés' casualties were two killed and twelve wounded. The Russians left fourteen dead and one seriously wounded in the tunnels, as well as an unknown number of dead and wounded groaning in no man's land.

On 17 September, Cuesta bid farewell to the 250th Reconnaissance Battalion and left for Viarlevo (Villa Relevo) in order to lead the 17th Return Battalion on its return to Spain. There he was joined by Posad's hero, Commander Tomás García Rebull.

Muñoz Grandes, doubting that von Manstein had enough strength left for Luz del Norte, sought to improve his defensive position before handing over the Division to Esteban Infantes, proposing to eliminate the salient of Iam Ishora, and so on September 29 he asked the 54th Army Corps for authorization to attack Putrolovo and Iam Ishora.

General Hansen was reluctant to do so, since it could warn the Russians about Operation Northern Light, since he did not know that this Operation was already dying. Muñoz Grandes' intuition had turned out to be true.

On the 12th of October, the feast of the Virgen del Pilar, most of the Portolés' Company had withdrawn to the rearguard in order to gather around the field kitchen that had arrived from Krasny Bor for breakfast, as things were relatively quiet. Suddenly, a barrage of cannon and mortar fire rained down on the positions. Throwing away their breakfast plates, the guripas tried to take cover, but before they could react, they began to receive rifle fire, machine-gun blasts and bombs from all sides. A battalion of the Russian 130th Regiment had gone on the attack. The cries of Urrah, Urrah, Ispankii Kaput! they were mixed with that of ¡Arriba España!; It was a tough situation, but the Spaniards managed to drive the Russians out of the trenches and hunt them down in no man's land. The counterattack was gaining momentum and Portolés and Arredondo led a group that came to the aid of two guripas who had fallen wounded about two hundred meters from the Russian trenches, but when they arrived next to them, they found themselves without ammunition. Then Arredondo began throwing clods at them as if they were hand bombs. A Russian officer stood up and smiled, running his index finger around his throat as he began to shoot them with his PPHS submachine gun. Arredondo jumped up with his machete and lunged at the red officer, but fell while in the air. Fortunately, the Portolés patrol arrived and rescued his wounded. Returning to their positions, the guripas made a silent prayer to the Virgen del Pilar, patron saint of all Spaniards.

The next morning Marshal von Manstein made an appearance in Pokrovskaia, where he was received with full honours by General Muñoz Grandes. Commander Collatz, head of the Liaison Detachment, translated the general's greeting and then Muñoz Grandes introduced General Esteban Infantes, Colonel Salazar, his chief of staff, his chief of operations Comandante Andino, and Captain Alemany, his chief of information. Then Muñoz Grandes took the Marshal and Commander Collatz to his office to have a long conversation while tasting coffee, cognac and cigars, all of which were almost impossible to obtain in Germany. While the conversation was going on, General Esteban Infantes and his staff moved nervously around the offices.

At the end of the conversation, von Manstein congratulated Muñoz Grandes for the splendid spirit of his men, evidenced by the heroic behavior of Portolés the day before, since it had been verified that the Russian dead exceeded one hundred, too many for a simple probation. Esteban Infantes and the others were then summoned for the obligatory photo and then von Manstein set off on his way back to Rozhdestveno.

On October 28 the Blue Division was ready and with a maximum capacity of 14,626 men, and two Marching Battalions were also on the way. The next day the 11th Army classified the 250th Division as an Attacking Division.

On November 8, the Allied invasion of North Africa began, and three days later, on the 19th, the Wehrmacht occupied Vichy France and the island of Corsica. The next day, General Franco ordered the mobilization of the 1941 and 1942 farms, with the intention of increasing the number of Army troops to 750,000 men. Three days later, the Berlin Embassy reported Hitler's intention to ask for passage through Spain. Consequently, Franco convened his cabinet and, after a long discussion, it was agreed that the Spanish government would reject the request. The next day, partial mobilization was decreed. Given the new problems he would face, Hitler believed that the return of Muñoz Grandes to Madrid was now imperative.

On December 2nd, the Count of Mayalde, ambassador in Berlin, and his substitute Vidal, went to the Wolf's Lair: Mayalde to say goodbye to Hitler and Vidal to present his credentials. In addition, Vidal was commissioned by Franco to request the return of Muñoz Grandes and to ask for the delivery of weapons, artillery and aircraft.

Determined to travel to Madrid, Muñoz Grandes visited Hitler and then flew to Berlin, where he visited the new Spanish Ambassador. On December 12, 1942, General Muñoz Grandes was ordered to return to Spain, despite the significant opposition of the Germans to his departure. And two days later Adolf Hitler imposed the Oak Leaves on his Knight's Cross of the Order of the Iron Cross, which he already owned. Command fell to the Division's second in command, General Emilio Esteban Infantes Martín.

Despite his wishes, on his arrival in Madrid he was enthusiastically received by thousands of people who cheered him on. In the next three days he was promoted to Lieutenant General.

On New Year's Eve, Franco invited him to dinner with the Minister of the Army, General Asensio, and then they had a long conversation about the latest events.

Meanwhile, in Russia, Christmas 1942 dawned black and threatening, although General Esteban Infantes, already more accustomed to it, decided to attack and Andino and Robles planned the operation.

On Wednesday, December 29, 1942, at 1:25 p.m., a real inferno broke out, as the batteries on all three sides of the salient began firing. More than five hundred grenades fell on the Russian positions in five minutes. Then, the firing was lengthened and under the order of "To the Assault" the 6th Company reached the enemy barbed wire, in which the sappers had already opened corridors and marked the minefields. The Soviets reacted weakly, the groups engaged in hand-to-hand combat while the sappers demolished the shelters with explosive charges, and the Russians began to flee on their feet. A green and white flare gave the signal for occupied position. The officers and sergeants called their men to return to their position, but they were reluctant and with combat fever wanted to continue to Kalinin. Then another orange flare gave the order "Mission accomplished, retreat" and the guripas began to retreat on their own lines, laden with booty and exhausted. The whole action had lasted 40 minutes: twelve pillboxes and three machine-gun nests had been destroyed and sixty Russians had perished, all at the cost of six guripas killed and nineteen wounded. A clean and seamless operation.

▲ Instruction of an engineer team, navigating a river and a dinghy, with an MG34 light machine gun and an explosives rod (BVD).

▲ Portrait of an artillery soldier from the mortar section of the 259th Artillery Regiment of the Blue Division (BVD).

▲ Portrait of a group of divisionaries next to a 150 mm FH 18 gun (BVD).

▼ Firing position of the MG 34 machine gun (BVD).

▲ Photograph of General Lindman being received at DA headquarters in Pokrowskaja, October '43 (BVD).

▼ Photograph of the DA drum band in Grigorowo, spring '42 (BVD).

▲ Obergefreiter Roberto Mericaechevarría Alcorta in oberschütze uniform with iron cross, holding an MP 40 machine gun.

▲ General Esteban Infantes reviews Spanish soldiers dressed in winter camouflage (NEG).

▼ General Kleffel's visit to the Spanish unit in 1943 (NEG).

▲ General Kleffel's visit to the DA. Spanish unit leader Emilio Esteban Infantes is seen (NEG).

▼ This meeting between the leaders of the DA and German General Kleffel took place on 14 September 1943 (NEG).

▲ Novgorov and Staraja Russa are cities etched in the history of Spanish soldiers on the Eastern Front (NEG).

▲ A Russian isba burning in the snowy landscape (NEG).

▼ The tough mission of some soldiers grappling with the fallen in combat (NEG).

▲ Spanish gunners prepare for next strike (NEG).

▲ Spanish soldiers pose for the camera (NEG).

▼ A group of DA soldiers in camouflage gear advances into Russian territory (NEG).

▲ Officers prepare their unit's next move on the Eastern Front (JAC).

▼ A Spanish soldier carries a 'gift of Caudillo Francisco Franco' box for the DA (JAC).

▲ Photograph of Captain Urbano Gómez García (BVD). At the top left, one can see the shield with the colours of the Spanish flag and the word 'Spain' at the top used by DEV men and LEV men on the right sleeve of their uniform. The Spaniards who continued fighting after the return of the LEV to Spain often kept this emblem, albeit on the left sleeve, as was customary in the Waffen SS. Public domain.

▲ A Spanish soldier posing smiling next to a cannon in winter camouflage (NEG).

▼ Several Soviet compatriots pose for the camera (NEG).

In the morning the new Chief of the Liaison Detachment, Lieutenant Colonel Wilhelm Knüppel, arrived. The Soviets initiated Operation Iskra, to liberate Leningrad from its encirclement, on the morning of January 12, 1943. More than 4,500 muzzles, including cannons, howitzers, mortars and rocket launchers, crushed the German defenses. The rough waves began to advance and Lindemann was forced to throw in his reserves, but the Russians continued to cling to the conquered ground. By January 16, the 18th Army was in dire straits, and all Lindemann had left was a narrow corridor. It was one kilometer wide and linked Sinevino to the shore of Lake Ladoga. The SS Polizei Division was withdrawn and the 250th was forced to turn right; the Spanish boundary would be three kilometers from the October Railway, on the Bol Izhorka River, which meant that the Krasny Bor sector would be extended to include the slope of the Moscow-Leningrad railway and half of the swamp between the embankment and the Tosna River, a total of five kilometers of new frontline.

Esteban Infantes ordered that the entire eastern sector be placed under the command of Colonel Sagrado. He abolished the Robles Group, as it would return to Spain very soon, and assigned the 262nd to the 250th Mobile Reserve Battalion, the Skier Company and the 2nd Divisional Anti-Tank Company. This sector comprised the area from Iam Izhora to the Tozna River. Commander Castro and his 1st of the 262nd replaced the Germans on the October Railway and in the peat bog to the East, while the 9th Battery joined Commander Reinhlein's 1st Group while Colonel Sagrado moved his HQ from Fedorovskoii to Krasny Bor and the 2nd of the 269th, commanded by Captain Patiño, He had left his positions and moved to the village of Pavlovsk, where he was kept as a reserve, but a few days later he was transferred as a reserve of the Army Corps to Sablino, where they arrived on the morning of January 17, 1943. Four days later, on the 21st, the 2nd of the 269th marched in trucks to Mga and Kelkolovo, where Patiño presented himself to General Werner Hühner of the 61st Division, receiving the order to join the 162nd Grenadier Regiment commanded by Colonel Vehrenkamp at Sinevino. Sinevino was in ruins. Fully loaded with all their impediments, the Spaniards crossed the destroyed streets and went into the forest in search of the 162nd Grenadiers. As soon as they found the exhausted Germans, they received word that the Russians had crossed the Kornaia and were infiltrating southwards. With such joyful news, the guripas greeted and continued their march.

After locating Colonel Vehrenkamp and advancing through the thicket, Captain Patiño finally joined his battalion and called a meeting of Officers, in order to inform them that the 2nd of the 269th was in the center of a gap in the German lines. They were at the front!

Despite the unknown terrain and the prevailing darkness, Patiño ordered the deployment and the 2nd of the 269th fanned out, looking for the 176th Grenadiers on the left and the 366th on the right. While the patrols scouted to the flanks, Captain Müller led the 6th Company on the left, Lieutenant Acosta took up position on horseback and east of the firebreak, and finally Captain Massip led the 7th Company on the right, while Captain Olmedo distributed his pieces: a section of machine guns to each of the Companies and the 81 mm mortars of the near the road, between the 5th and 6th Companies.

There were no fortifications. The guripas began to collect timber and branches, piling them on parapets, facing north, and covering them with snow. However, it didn't take long for the infiltrated Russians to start the packing from the South. Not far from the road and behind the 5th Company, six shallow pillboxes were located, in which the Pater (Chaplain) and the doctors were placed, who very soon began to be very busy, as the initial trickle of wounded soon turned into a torrent as dawn approached. At six o'clock in the morning, the Soviet 11th and 71st divisions opened fire with everything they had: cannons, howitzers, rocket launchers, anti-tank pieces and mortars, and the tremendous fire, lasting two and a half hours, fell on the 2nd of the 269th and the 366th Wehrmacht Grenadiers.

The makeshift snow shelters vanished almost immediately. At dawn, about nine o'clock, the positions of Müller and Acosta were clearly in view, and Massip's, more advanced and on open ground, was completely exposed. The Russians, protected under cover, aimed directly and an anti-tank shot hit the Spaniards, causing deaths and mutilations. Unable to take it any longer, Müller and Acosta took their men to a shelter in the woods. The Russians began the attack by launching several infantry regiments, but the Spaniards of the 5th and 6th Companies held on, but again came back to the charge again and again: they bombed, attacked and retreated and so on throughout the day. By about noon, more than a hundred guripas and half a dozen officers had fallen. The wounded, after emergency treatment, returned to their fighting posts or were sent to the rear aboard sledges.

Massip had reached the link up with Wengler and his Westphalians troops shortly before dawn and received two machine guns with his crews to complete the Ensign Casas´ Section of the 8th Company, but he did not have enough strength to be able to cover his entire Sector. Massip did everything he could and organized his defenses on islets, in the Spanish manner. Soviet artillery took a tremendous toll. Massip was wounded by shrapnel in the forehead, but he ignored it and continued to slide from one pit to another encouraging his men. At dawn on Friday, while Massip was making his rounds, a Russian regiment came out into the open field shouting "Urrah, Urrah!" and then the Spanish machine guns began to sing. Russian corpses piled up in front of the fragile Spanish front, but they kept trying again and again, managing to isolate the 7th Company. The shooter of a machine gun collapsed dead and Massip sat in the saddle and opened fire, but a bullet hit him in the left eye, but he kept firing as a bloody pulp slid over his cheek and froze. The guripas shouted at him, "Back, my Captain," but he refused. A doctor put a bandage over his face and continued shooting, but another shot hit him in the right leg. His men shouted again, "Back, my Captain," but he shook his head negatively. Unable to walk, he crawled along a line. The 2nd Section had disappeared, blown to pieces during the last bombardment. Abrain and Casas had been killed, as were five of the German machine gunners, but Alemany was trying to plug the gaps in the line by reattaching his remaining machine guns.

Now the Russians were coming in slower, small groups were gliding through the clearing, but there were no more mass assaults. Night was coming and the enemy's advance guard was only twenty yards away and only a few cartridges remained. Painfully on his feet, Massip drew the safety of his last grenade and died as he threw it, for a burst struck him full with his last command: "Put bayonets."

The news began to reach Patiño's HQ and the wounded whispered among themselves that the 7th Company was still holding on. But Verheinkamp ordered a counterattack, so forming a wedge with the two hundred guripas he had left, Patiño led them in their attack at midnight and a fierce hand-to-hand fight ensued, with the 5th and 6th Companies reconquering their positions.

By the end of the day on Saturday, January 23, contact with Massip's men had been restored. The 7th Company was still holding out, but Wengler, finding himself harassed, ordered them out as he had to retreat. Carrying their weapons, their wounded, and the corpse of Captain Massip covered with a blanket, the surviving guripas passed into the immediate reserve, behind the 336th Grenadiers.

Sunday began as a day of rest. Nonetheless, the Soviets had reinforced themselves with the 349th Infantry Division in order to shore up the punished 11th and 71st Divisions. Luckily, Lieutenant Soriano had appeared, and when Verheinkamp called for thirty men to re-establish the line, Soriano led his Section, of the 6th Company, into the breach.

On Monday, it was Patiño's turn to operate with a section, but he was wounded. The bleeding continued. On the 26th, a direct hit on the Command Post injured 6 officers, a sergeant, and five guripas. And so on for three more days.

Finally, on Saturday, January 30, the relief order was received. At 8:30 a.m., the 2nd of the 269th formed and emerged from the gloomy forests of Sinevinus. The guripas climbed into a lonely truck, for there was plenty of room. When they finally reached their destination, Paulovsk, only one officer, six sergeants and twenty guripas did so, so the total casualties suffered in the Second Battle of Lake Ladoga had been 124 killed, 211 wounded, 92 missing, 66 with frostbite and 12 sick.

Marshal von Küchler arrived at the 50th Army Headquarters at Taitsy on 6 February, as he was sure that the 51st Red Army would attack the thin Spanish lines with heavy artillery preparation, as it had done south of Lake Ladoga, and then penetrate the defences with its tanks and infantry. And then, pessimistically, he left for Pokrovskaia. For his part, General Esteban Infantes was confident, but what was expected was nothing reassuring. Then, in a message to the sector commanders, he ordered all the anti-aircraft guns to be taken out of the front line, except those on the islets, and to be placed in the immediate rear. Likewise, each Company would withdraw four new machine guns, preferably heavy, as it expected that the artillery concentration would be concentrated in the front line, and wanted to salvage as much as it could in order to be able to respond adequately to the next assault.

For his part, Kleffel ordered Esteban Infantes to send the Sappers, the anti-tank guns and the 11th Battery to the Sagrado Sector. And he also ordered the transfer of his HQ from Novolisino to the southeast of Krasny Bor, as well as that the SS Polizei Division should fall back between the 250th and the 5th Mountain Divisions, because, although severely punished, it still showed itself to be strong.

The rally in Krasny Bor continued. The arrival of the additional batteries required a higher-ranking commander, for which Bandin appointed Santos, his deputy, who assumed command of Reinlhein's 1st Group and the 9th and 11th Batteries. When the 150 mm pieces arrived, the 105 mm ones advanced individually to a support line, where they could make direct fire against the Russians.

Rumours of the Russian offensive were true and so on 9 February the Soviets proceeded to blow up their own minefields off Krasny Bor and then, in small groups, set about removing those that had not exploded. Bandin ordered to open fire and the Spanish artillery began to cannonade Kolpino, but the Reds did not design to respond. By nightfall the front was calm, with the exception of Spanish artillery fire on Kolpino. When Captain Oroquieta had just entered his HQ, Lieutenant Bleza, from Transmissions, an old friend whom he had not seen since the time of the civil war, burst in. He arrived accompanied by four German technicians carrying telephone interception equipment with which Russian communications could be listened to and which they then set up near the Soviet outposts. Soon they began using the 2nd Company's radio to report their discoveries to Division Headquarters.

On his return to Prokovskaia, Lieutenant Alemany reported the information he had obtained. The prisoners' statements, the artillery tests, the blowing up of mines, and now the intercepted telephone messages, made it clear that the Russian attack would begin the next day on Krasny Bor.

Consequently, the Units were alerted so that they could be prepared for what was going to happen tomorrow. At midnight, the Pater Pumariño appeared in the trench of Oroquieta, who, like most of his one hundred and ninety-six guripas, confessed and received communion and then they went to their positions in order to be able to sleep a little. Around 2 a.m. the ringing of the telephone woke up Oroquieta, it was Ulzurrun, who had just returned from a reconnaissance in which they had surprised a Russian patrol that was dedicated to cutting communications cables, killing some and capturing the Lieutenant who commanded it, who was reluctant to talk.

Captain Palacios could not restrain his anger, for the explosions and detonators for the hand grenades and mines had not yet arrived.

At dawn the sky was clear and nothing was visible in front of it, but the artillery observers' telescopes discovered thirteen KV-1s and T-34s advancing towards the positions of the 5th and 6th Companies. The sergeants and corporals issued the order: "All to the pillboxes except those at the post." At the end of the line, Captain Losada's 1st Company took charge of the situation while coldly watching forty Russian tanks arriving from Kolpino to take up positions on either side of the October Railway. Suddenly, a red flare rose into the sky from the Soviet lines. It was 6:45 a.m. on February 10, 1943, and then eight hundred muzzles began to spit fire on the lines of Colonel Sagrado. The earth was shaking and moving. Frisian horses, with dangling barbed wire, were flying through the air and a moonscape was being created. The Spanish artillery responded as fast as it could, as did the German batteries, but they were tremendously outnumbered. The sergeants circulated among the guripas cheering them on and handing out brandy, since it was bitterly cold: 30 degrees below zero.

Casualties were still few in the 3rd Company. Huidobro arrived from the anti-tank observation post, because although the telephone link with Commander Castro's HQ was cut off, he still had a line to the batteries. He had just called for artillery fire when the Reds began to concentrate in front of the positions of Captains Iglesia and Palacio. Meanwhile Iglesias was dead.

Sweating despite the bitter cold, the gunners of the 1st Group charged and fired at an incredible rate. No one thought about resting. Leaning over the table in the command fort, Reinlhein strained his ears to catch the messages coming from the advanced observatories, for although most of the telephone lines had been shredded, some radios were still broadcasting. Behind Reinlhein, near the entrance, stood Lieutenant Colonel Santos and his staff. Suddenly, a deafening explosion ensued: Santos, a captain and three lieutenants were riddled with shrapnel from the red projectile.

The 1st and 2nd Companies at "Panzer Peak" were desperately asking for artillery support, but some of Reinlhein's howitzers had been blown to pieces. The fortifications of Losada and Muñoz had disintegrated at the first blow of the Russian hammer.

Huidobro was dedicated to recovering the retreaters, many of whom were wounded and some unarmed, but all of them were obfuscated. He selected them and sent the slightly wounded to the trenches along the slope. Some refused to stop, rookie soldiers (named "Mortadelas") fleeing for safety.

General Esteban Infantes had spent a sleepless night. The booms of Russian artillery spread to the south, gleaming in the dark windows of the palace. Shortly after 6:45 a.m., Captain Calvo called from the 3rd of the 262nd to confirm the intensity of the cannonade. The General, seated at his table, listened. An hour passed, and the dispatch still reverberated with the Russian artillery fire.

At about 8 a.m., the buzz seemed to change. Esteban Infantes was convinced that the main attack was aimed at Krasny Bor. The General asked for a car and left for the observation post at Raikolovo, followed by an escort car. When they were close to Pavlovsk, a curtain of fire covered the road, so they had to turn in the direction of Antropshino, from where a secondary road led to Fedorovskii, Raikolovo and Antropshino, the latter seeming to be on fire. In order to reduce the chances of Russian artillery inflicting more casualties, platoons began to slide eastward toward the Division's provisional headquarters.

Pushing his way, the General reached Raikolovo, where an advanced hospital was on fire and many of its patients had received new wounds. Esteban Infantes ordered the hospital staff to leave for the South, to Ladoga, and then returned to their temporary HQ.

Colonel Sagrado telephoned with unreassuring reports. His HQ was hit regularly. Santos had been killed and Reinlhein was taking his place, ordering each battery to zero out against half a dozen Russian tanks that had overtaken his infantry and were raiding the northern rim of Krasny Bor. There was no news of the Izhora, but it was known that Ulzurrún had died leading a last, futile counterattack. Miranda was desperately trying to plug the gap where the 2nd Company had been. The HQ of the 2nd Battalion was almost surrounded, and Payerás was dying. Little was known of Castro, but Russian infantry and armor were advancing toward "Panzer Peak." There were still some pockets on the front line. The advanced observatories distinguished four islets: Oroquieta on the Moscow-Leningrad highway; Campos with elements of the 6th, 7th and 8th Companies, together with the 2nd Anti-Tank Company, in "El Bastion"; Aramburu with the 3rd Sappers on the road behind "El Bastión" and Palacios and Huidobro along the embankment. Thus, the Spaniards clung everywhere to the high ground, forming islands of resistance in an emerging Red steam-roller. The news were confusing because the fast movement of troops. The second line held out and three new islets, garrisoned mainly by the 2nd Squadron, were backing the remaining four in the old main line of resistance. Captain Cantalapiedra had set up his tank destroyers in front of Captain Andrés' 1st Battery and had managed to destroy four tanks at point-blank range. Colonel Sagrado informed General Esteban Infantes of this momentary success, but the General was sure that the Red horde would return again stronger than before, sweeping away the defenders. Almost desperately, he thought that all might be lost, and hoped that Heckel would be able to arrive in time with the 390th Grenadier to prevent the slaughter.

The 55th Red Army did not give up and shortly afterwards some tanks and infantry overwhelmed Payerás's HQ and Butler's forward observation post, managing to penetrate Krasny Bor. Avoiding the strong points, they headed straight for the Colonel Sagrado's Command Post. Cornered, sacred, he personally led a counterattack. Jumping from the sappers' command post, about two hundred meters in front of the regimental HQ, they managed to push the Russians back some five hundred meters beyond the emplacements of the 1st Battery, managing to free some Spanish prisoners in the process, but the positions previously recaptured by the 2nd Squadron had been lost. Captain Andujar had fallen with his riders. The Russian infantry, who were infiltrating the pockets, groped him with the bayonet, leaving him for dead, but when the counterattack reached its height, he painfully rose to his feet and joined it.

Colonel Sagrado summoned Commanders Reinlhein, of the 1st Group, and Bellod, of the 250th Sappers. Exhausted and obfuscated, the Colonel decided to leave direct command to both of them. Reinlhein was to take charge of the section from the Moscow-Leningrad highway to Sovietskii Street, and Bellod, from the main street, to the east, to Popovka. Sagrado then informed both of them that a German regiment was coming from Sablino and, since all contact with Raikolovo had been cut off. He was going to march to the rear to try to telephone General Esteban Infantes. The Colonel left for the 2nd Battery and when he arrived at the settlement of his 155 mm Schneider pieces (from those captured by the Wehrmatch in France), he discovered that the gunners had also lost their communications, so he decided to try the powder magazine in the forest, behind Krasny Bor. In the meantime, the defense continued, but... without the Colonel.

Reinlhein and Bellod took care of everything immediately. Withdrawing their advanced elements about a hundred yards, they established a new line along the heights that extended just north of the city center. On the left Reinlhein gathered what was left of the 2nd Squadron, disoriented 5th and 6th Companies, lost guripas of the 250th Reserve Battalion, and uncommanded anti-tankers. Almost the only intact unit he had was Commander

La Cruz's Assault Section, but it was somewhere to the west.

Bellod, based his defenses on what was left of the 1st and 2nd Sapper Companies and aided by Commander Castro, who had managed to escape, Captain Rodrigo and Lieutenant Frago, created a line to the East. A hard fight had been waged over the railway bridge near the Stepanonka-Chernyshevo-Nikolsloie road, where Mankhon had been hit, but support was needed. By picking up retreating men from the 1st of the 262nd, the 3rd Squadron and the gunners were able to consolidate a front that ran from Butler's 2nd Battery, opposite the fort of Bellod on the other side of the October Railway, and continued past Popovka Station. There, Captain Lopez, whose 150mm pieces of his 11th Battery were still pulling, swelled his ranks with the bewildered guripas who drifted past. A perimeter defense company of the Wehrmacht's 138th Artillery Unit, commanded by Lieutenant Loppel, reinforced its command by taking over the defense of Popovka station.

The Russians kept pressing, but their attacks lacked the previous verve. Having checked out his new devices, Reinlein began to radio all the remaining islets in the western sector. At eleven o'clock he spoke to the 3rd Sappers and Aramburu told him that a new attack had just been repulsed. The assault sappers on the El Bastion road, as well as their comrades on Krasny Bor, had seen the artillery barrage rise at 9:30 a.m. Fifteen minutes later, when Campos gave way, two tanks and a large number of Russian infantry rushed into Aramburu's flank. One KV-1 got stuck in a minefield, which had been planted the night before, and flew into the air, causing the other to retreat. Then there was a pause during which Campos and Arozarena, with what was left of the 6th, 7th, and 8th Companies at El Bastion, managed to make contact with Aramburu. Taking advantage of the Soviet standstill, more mines were planted, especially on the flanks, but there were very few left to place on the road, so Aramburu ordered his empty boxes to be scattered there, trusting that this would serve to divert the tanks arriving from Iam Izhora, where Oroquieta was still resisting.

The machine gunners of "La Tía Bernarda" had managed to decimate the 133rd Regiment when it attacked the positions of Captain Ulzurrún and when they retreated a Section launched a counterattack. Ulzurrún walked through what was left of the bastions encouraging his men with the Falangist cry of "Arriba España" and the legionnaire with "Long live death!", but a bullet hit him in the shoulder, so holding his paralyzed arm with the other hand, he put it in a pocket, trusting that the cold would close the wound and stop the bleeding. Suddenly, twenty guripas from the sector's reserve crawled in, they were the survivors of the 1st Company, which Miranda, although wounded, had led in two counterattacks in order to stop the 133rd Regiment and the 14th Regiment that followed him, but Miranda had died during his second counterattack. These regiments then began a turn towards the Izhora, where they suffered a devastating attack with hand bombs by Lieutenant Caraballo's assault sapper platoon, which caused the Russians to head towards the 150 mm howitzers of the 13th Company commanded by Captain Díez Miranda, who defended their positions until the end. He and Caraballo gained time that they paid for with their lives. The Soviets had paid a very high price for this, estimated at 65% to 75% casualties, although they nevertheless managed to reach the river, in the vicinity of Staraia Myza.

Captain Oroquieta had just been cut off on the left and rear, and he had lost most of his officers, and his battered pillboxes were overflowing with wounded he could not evacuate. All that remained was seventy guripas and a machine gun in Oroquieta. The Russian artillery extended the fire while five T-34s launched themselves against the Spaniards and broke through the line. To the north, the infantry made an appearance, advancing "en masse". Oroquieta ordered to open fire and the Russians began to pile up and then retreated, but later attacked again, but this time with mortar and anti-tank fire, thus wiping out the last machine gun they had left. By the time, Campos had retired, leaving the right side off. Stoically, Oroquieta watched the long columns of red infantry, piercing through the gap in close order. The Spaniards were constantly firing on their bare flank, but the impassive Russians continued to march towards Krasny Bor. Finally, Oroquieta concentrated the few men he had left on horseback from the high ground, on the road. It was already 10:30 a.m.

From his position, Oroquieta watched sadly as a column of Spanish prisoners marched towards the Russian rearguard. Their rescue was out of the question, for their small company was surrounded on all sides. After intense, but brief mortar fire, the Soviets launched their third mass attack. Only rifles and hand grenades remained for the Spaniards, but they were enough, since the 12th Battery opened fire from Fedorovskii and hit them squarely causing carnage among the compact Russian ranks, but Oroquieta had been wounded again, this time in the right leg.

"The time has come for heroic decisions," General Esteban Infantes said, forcing a confident smile and hiding his emotions and apprehensions, he continued: "We must do all we can to protect that flank on the Izhora, for since it is impossible to reinforce Krasny Bor, we will send the reserves there and let the Krasny Bor forces hold on as best they can."

Lieutenant Colonel Robles understood that this was his turn, since the entire sector had been his for months. Araujo was new and Sagrado was not up to par. An old and worthy comrade-in-arms, Cano, of the 269th, would take care of the Izhora while he tried to save the rest. Alemany had gone to Krasny Bor to take a look and would soon return with the impression achieved.

Oroquieta continued to cling to the road, enduring sporadic attacks accompanied by mortar fire. Suddenly, during one of the pauses, a drunken Russian appeared on the road from the south and went straight to the Spanish positions, proudly showing the guripas two bottles of brandy and a pile of cigarettes, the product of the booty. Oroquieta tried to interrogate him, but the Russian was so drunk that he had to be allowed to "sleep during the hangover" in a trench, where he fell asleep. Ammunition was already scarce and not a single hand bomb remains.

Time was also running out for Captain Palacios, who was also almost out of ammunition and with many wounded concentrated in the only remaining fort.

To the shouts of the sentries, they came out of the fort and the Russians were already lying down, Castillo fired the last magazine of his MP-38/41 and a few fell, but they were surrounded. One of the Russians hit was lying moaning and a non-commissioned officer asked him if he could hold on, but turning his head he told him no, and then the sergeant raised his pistol and shot him in the back of the head. "Prisoners", Palacios thought, "and if they are able to do this to their own, what will they do to our wounded?" Then, as they left the trench, the night closed behind the small column of 35 Spanish prisoners, of whom 21 were wounded.

The Russians once more regained their position at Oroquieta, but were again repulsed, although Blesa, their childhood friend, was hit in the forehead by a bullet that killed him instantly. The captain counted his men again: thirteen, five of them wounded, but still standing. It was all that was left of the 250th Mobile Reserve Battalion. While waiting for nightfall, to try to escape, the Russians appeared by surprise pointing guns at the Spaniards. They had been taken prisoner.

Already three of the four pockets of resistance (Altura, Palacios and Oroquieta) had been extinguished. Only the islet of Aramburu remained. By the time Campos and Arozarena fell back from El Bastion, he had been tasked with defending the rear. Aramburu now had enough to keep his bulwark above the road. And he had enough officers to retain the integrity of command. After a few unsuccessful attacks, the Russians turned away from them. At 3:30 a.m., a transmission team arranged for Krasny Bor to rewire the cable and re-establish telephone communications, but, surprised by a Russian column, they were forced to retreat and the same thing happened again in a later attempt. Disappointed, but not discouraged, Aramburu knew that Reinlein was still in the city.

Commanders Reinlein and Bellod had had a very eventful Wednesday afternoon. While the Russians paused to reinforce and regroup, the infantry engaged in plunder. Deprived of the bulk of their covering troops, the tank crews hesitated until the officers and commissars managed to control them, and at noon they set off again. In the meantime, the two Commanders had managed to stabilize the situation, although there was no choice but to blow up the pieces of the 11th Battery. La Cruz was on its way with what was left of its Assault Section. He was coming through the Red Forest, and there, on the log road, he met a mixed group of uncommanded guripas, whose honor had prevented him from retiring any further. Separating the wounded, he sent the rest to the rear, to Raikolovo.

The guripas of the 1st and 3rd Batteries were fighting for their lives. Very important explosions smashed the streets of Krasny Bor. The guripas fired from windows and doors at the infiltrated Russians. Others were kicking from the rooftops. The Sappers, as in the civil war, threw hand bombs and gasoline bottles on the T-34 and KV-1, managing to set some of them on fire.

Jumping into the sidecar of his motorcycle, Reinlein went out to the powder keg, where luckily a telephone still worked. At about 3:15 p.m. he met with General Esteban Infantes and was able to inform him in detail of the chaos that reigned in Krasny Bor. For his part, the General announced that the Luftwaffe was on its way and that the Heckel Battle Group would arrive at any moment. Overjoyed by the news, he jumped back on the bike and set off along the Moscow-Leningrad highway in search of the German tip, which was approaching at the junction of the road to Raikolovo.

Reinlein introduced himself to Colonel Heckel to inform him of the news. As the new head of the sector. Pointing to the map, the Commander proudly proclaimed that the 1st and 3rd Batteries were still in action and were now centers of resistance. Morale was high, despite the casualties, and would rise even as the Spaniards saw their fellow Germans arrive. In addition, he told her that, if he ordered her to, he would love to lead a counterattack. The Colonel replied that he already had a battalion on the road and another in the woods, there was the Northeast, in order to link up with the Spanish defenses at Krasny Bor. He had previously sent Lieutenant Ulric to the city to establish contact, but Ulric found not Spaniards, but Russians everywhere. Heckel then told Reinlein that he was "astonished to have found on the road Spanish soldiers returning to Sablino." Reinlein replied that "all the officers of those soldiers had been wounded or were dead." Then, after these defenses of the honor of his countrymen, he returned to the 1st Battery. Reinlein observed that the Germans had advanced about 300 meters and then stopped, then dug in. It was clear that Heckel was not going to link up with Aramburu, with himself, or with Bellod. The German Colonel seemed content to creep to the edge of the forest and gaze at Krasny Bor. Once again, whether he liked it or not, Reinlein was in charge. Two Colonels had failed him: one Spanish and one German.

The Colonel Sagrado, who had returned to Krasny Bor, once again left Reinlein alone. He then headed west with part of his Staff, and then south through the forest of Sablino in search of the 390th Grenadiers. After advancing a kilometer between snow-covered trees, he was intercepted by a German patrol, which took him another two kilometers to Sablino, where his Battalion was located, and then headed towards Heckel's HQ, but he was unable to locate him, so he turned north again, to Krasny Bor, where he met Lieutenant Vega, whom he ordered to go to the crossroad of the wood road with the Moscow-Leningrad road. And in contrast to what might have been expected, Colonel Sagrado turned around and left for Sablino to confer with General Reymann of the 212th Division, who had taken over command of the entire Sector.

At 4:30 a.m., Kleffel notified Esteban Infantes that Reymann had taken command of the Sector, from the Izhora to the October Railway. The 316th Grenadier Regiment would be deployed between the river and the road. Heckel, now attached to the 212th Division, would remain between the Segura and the railroad.

Kleffel didn't seem to notice that Aramburu, Reinlein, and Bellod were still holding out. Although he had Alemany's direct report, General Esteban Infantes was unable to communicate with the head of the Army Corps, as all he knew was that the officers of "Villa Relevo" who had tried to reach Krasny Bor by the log road, had died while trying to re-establish communications. All the General knew for sure was that the large Soviet force threatening the road was approaching Chernaia Rechka and his HQ at Raikolovo.

Robles and Cano did what they could. With the Reds facing Raikolovo, the western escape route for the wounded and the scattered from Krasny Bor was cut off. This advance also endangered the rear of the White Battalion, of the 263rd on the other side of the Izhora. Moreover, the Army Corps insisted that the Spaniards hold on to Staraia Myza. When Cano had informed Robles, the sector chief explained that they could not expect any more forces from the 263rd or 269th. Their lines had so little consistency that a single Russian blow could pierce them.

Lieutenant Colonel Robles had surrounded Raikolovo with the mortars and machine guns of the 4th Company of the 263rd and the 8th of the 269th, as well as reinforced the perimeter with the only Section of the 7th Company of the 269th. The 9th of the 263rd should arrive around three o'clock in the afternoon and Robles would like to be able to use them as a reserve for the subsector if he could persuade Esteban Infantes to dispense with the protection of his HQ. To the north, in Podolovo, there were only transmission, quartermaster and health personnel. Beyond, in Samsonovka, the situation was chaotic. Alemany had gone there and said that scattered officers and soldiers were prowling the town for no apparent purpose. On the other hand, Alemany had failed to obtain information from Commander White, who was fighting on the other side of the river, in Staraia Myza.

Lieutenant Colonel Cano departed from Raikolovo to scout his new sub-sector of the Izhora, He knew that the 3rd of the 262nd had an old and well-established front, but he was not unaware that this battalion had suffered 40% casualties from artillery fire. He first checked the condition of the 14th Company of the 262nd and the 3rd Artillery Group, at Moiskropovo; then he did it in the paper mill, where Captain Ortega was supported, behind its high walls, with the 1st Reconnaissance Squadron and groups of guripas and artillerymen. As he crossed the great meander of the Izhora he found himself in the middle of an intense barrier fire, which did not affect him. He continued on to the 7th battery and found his four pieces throwing steel at a compact mass that was attacking across the icy river and being forced back. He finally went to Araujo's HQ, where he was informed that Staraia Myza had just fallen. The 1st Battalion of the 263rd was returning from the other side of the Izhora, but where was Commander Blanco? No one knew.

Without returning to his HQ, Lieutenant Colonel Blanco, with the help of Captains Urbano and La Fuente and Lieutenant Garcia, rallied the Guripas into a line of defense around Samsonovka. When the Lieutenant Colonel was finally able to return to his HQ, he met the Commander Blanco who had just arrived: he was the last Spaniard to leave Staraia Myza alive.

The large Soviet rally was taking place in front of Samsonovka. Cano asked Robles to dispense with the reserves in Raikolovo, to which Esteban Infantes agreed. However, part of the 9th of the 263rd remained there for defense and another Section marched to the log road. Robles had already sent a patrol, accompanied by the Prince of Metternich, interpreter of General Esteban Infantes, along the route: there was not the slightest presence of Reds or Germans. Where was the 390th Grenadiers? A few heroes held out on the heights and the remaining pieces of the 1st and 3rd Batteries continued to fire. Reinlein had just returned to Captain Andrew's fort when the Russians unleashed a new attack. Tanks and swarms of soldiers were coming down the Sovietskii Street in a southerly direction. The Guripas were defenseless against the KV-1s. Hiding among the ruined buildings, they waited until they passed and then fought the infantry.

Lieutenant Constantino Goduidionachvili was with Commander Bellod, who had just returned from a reconnaissance of El Bastion, when the attack began. Given the irruption, the former Tsarist Captain and Civil War fighter enlisted in The Legion, had been trying to help maintain the second line. He was discussing the situation with Commander Bellod when a KV-1 turned the corner of Sovietskii Street firing cannon and machine gun. Captain Muñoz García also saw him coming, who ordered his sappers to sow the street with T mines (Tellermine), but the tank leader, cautious as he did not have infantry in support, turned towards the Hospital, located in a two-story building near the Regiment's Communist Party. The KV-1 was heading straight for the door of the Hospital, firing constantly. Some guripas tried to stop him with Molotov cocktails and sticking magnetic mines that did not cause him the slightest damage. Suddenly, the sapper Antonio Ponte Anido, Commander Bellod's liaison, slipped loaded with two T mines to the KV-1 and threw them under his belly and a tremendous explosion ended the KV-1, but also his life. At five o'clock in the afternoon it was calm in Krasny Bor, although small clashes persisted, but the artillery was silent.

Bellod had had enough. Colonel von Below, wasting no time, had sent the 374th Grenadier from Sablino by the October Railway, and was formed up behind him, and immediately deployed them, placing them eastward on the heights. Bellod, upon being informed that the 390th and 374th Regiments were in charge of command, withdrew what was left of the 250th Reconnaissance, the 1st of the 262nd and the Combat Sappers, leaving Sablino at 6:30 p.m.

Seeing Bellod marching, Lieutenant Jobst, of the Liaison Commission, became uneasy, as Heckel's Battle Group should have been there for hours, so he decided to look for his HQ and left Popovka heading west. At last, after an hour's walk, he met Heckel in the woods, south of the Orthodox Church, who informed him that his 390th Regiment was in position and that he had already taken charge of the sector.

There was already a new line along the forest, from the Moscow-Leningrad highway to the east to the SS Polizei Division. However, having no news from the Division, Reinlein and La Cruz were reluctant to retreat and in addition, guripas who had been in hiding were arriving, both in small groups and alone from El Trincherón and did not want to abandon Aramburu, who was isolated in the north of the Red Forest.

Robles was advancing along the log road, for when news of the disappearance of the Sacred Colonel leaked out, he left Raikolovo for Krasny Bor with a Squadron and a small Staff. By the side of the road, in a cabin, he set up his HQ. Unfortunately, the 262nd no longer existed, but the veteran legionnaire rounded up the fugitives and displaced people and deployed them in a line along the upper edge of the Red Forest. There, between the Izhora and the Moscow-Leningrad Highway, there would be a big gap. The 316th Regiment was to come from Sablino, but until it arrived and formed a stronger line, the Division and the Army Corps were in high danger.

Lindemann telephoned Esteban Infantes and as Metternich translated for him, he reported. Then Lindemann replied bluntly: "Staraia Myza must be preserved unconditionally. Together with the 316th Grenadiers, it will attack to the north."

Robles was very eager to perform with the 316th, but he couldn't wait. By 9 p.m. he had managed to gather enough guripas to form a company, but there was a lack of officers, the services were scarce and they had no automatic weapons. He had convinced his artillerymen without howitzers, his infantrymen without weapons, and his cooks without kitchens, that powerful German forces had clung to each of their flanks and that they were really in the second line. But naturally he thought otherwise, for it seemed certain that the Russian 72nd Division was going to attack the next morning. One of his sentinels gave him the news that a column was approaching from the Log Road in close order. The voices that could be heard were neither German nor Spanish, but the steel helmets seemed to be their own. Lieutenant Colonel Robles came out and, raising a hand, called a halt. They were Estonians and their Captain explained to him, in broken German, that they were two companies of the 658th Battalion, sent to take charge of the defense of the perimeter of the 138th Artillery Group, since several German batteries had been exposed. And he asked Robles if he could guide them, but the latter, pretending not to understand, invited the captain to his hut. There, by candlelight, the Lieutenant Colonel, who knew very well that the German batteries were three kilometers away, pointed out on his map "the real situation", so that the Estonians would have to deploy along the border of the Red Forest, between the Izhora and the Moscow-Leningrad Highway. The Estonian captain came out and gave some orders. The gap was closed.

The Colonel Sagrado was safe in Sablino. He had arrived at about 7 a.m. and immediately requested an interview with General Reymann, but the commander of the 212th Division did not wish to see him and kept him waiting for more than three hours. Meanwhile, Sagrado telephoned Esteban Infantes and told the General that "his command post had been destroyed by Russian tank fire and occupied by the Red infantry." This claim was refuted by Lieutenant Jobst, the regiment's liaison officer. "Lacking any means of assistance," continued the Colonel, "he had sought Heckel in the south, whose arrival had been announced and who might have advanced, but did not. In reality, an early intervention would not only have supported his Spanish forces, but would also have been useful in sustaining the sector." It was not until Bellod arrived at Popovka that he knew for sure that his men were still holding out.

When Sagrado was finally ushered into General Reymann's room, the reception was very cold. Jobst, who had come from Heckel's HQ, served as interpreter, Reymann instructed Sagrado to remain in Sablino. He was not going to return to Raikolovo, but would stay and help round up the fugitives and displaced people. He also informed him that Esteban Infantes had sent Lieutenant Fernandez from his General Staff to take over the command. Moreover, Reymann declined to employ reorganized Spanish units in his sector. The interview ended. The Colonel Sagrado was scrapped, but overcame it enough to send more ammunition to Reinlein on Krasny Bor. This was his last order as Colonel commanding the 262nd Regiment.

Reinlein and La Cruz were suffering more from the German bombing than from the Soviet bombing and had not seen a fugitive or displaced person for hours and still had no news from the Division, but they were already sure that the Germans had taken charge of the situation. It was time to leave.

After blowing up their only remaining piece, a Howitzer of the 105th, Commander Reinlein and Captain Andrés left the islet around the 1st Battery, along with about fifty artillerymen. They were followed by Commander La Cruz and Captain Apestegui with almost a hundred anti-tankers and infantrymen. The small column passed the Hospital, its battered regimental HQ, the ruined Orthodox church, and was approaching the log road, when a German Lieutenant emerged from the shadows who wished to speak to the Commanding Officer. Reinlein and La Cruz took the lead. The translator was in trouble, and as he struggled, the Spaniards noticed the bright red badges on their warrior's collar. He was an artilleryman and undoubtedly wanted them to stay. Its 155 mm battery. It was located south of the Sablino forest and if the Spaniards left, its pieces would be fully exposed to an assault by the Soviet infantry and in this case, it would be forced to blow them up.

La Cruz refused, Reinlein, who had suffered the agony of defending his Howitzers all day and finally blowing them up, hesitated, for here was a comrade artilleryman in desperate straits. Besides, Aramburu could be alive. He nodded, and La Cruz tried to dissuade him, but failed. The anti-tankers marched south towards Sablino, while Reinlein, Andrew, and their fifty artillerymen dug in before the German battery. It was now a little after midnight. Black Wednesday, February 10, 1943, was over.

Aramburu, along with Captains Campos and Arozarena, had decided to try to make the exit. Krasny Bor was calm. There had been a commotion at the Izhora around eleven o'clock, but it had been two hours of that time. The three officers feared that the Red Army had swept everything away and marched towards Sablino, so they destroyed everything they could not carry, then loaded the wounded onto sledges and headed for the road, for Aramburu came to the conclusion that this was the fast and direct mass route to the rear. Preceded by reconnaissance patrols, the almost two hundred men belonging to the 3rd Sapper Companies, the 7th and 8th of the 262nd and 3rd of "La Tía Bernarda", undertook the march to the South, but were discovered and attacked, but managed to elude enemy action. Finally, about four kilometers from their starting point, they met the Anti-Tank Assault Section and slowly continued on to Sablino, beginning to meet soldiers of the 390th Regiment, whom Aramburu asked for their Colonel's HQ. When Aramburu introduced himself to Heckel, he immediately realized that Heckel was not satisfied, but rather surprised, for he believed that there were no Spaniards in Krasny Bor.

When Reinlein and Aramburu withdrew, the 55th Red Army came behind and reached its immediate objective; the southern edge of Krasny Bor. To the west, the 72nd Division had won the Izhora. To the east, the 43rd Division was advancing on Nikolskoye. But the Russian attack had not stalled, as the surviving units of the high ground and the new islets established by the mid-morning counterattack disoriented the Soviet momentum. The generals of the Red Army were very surprised that anyone had been left alive because of their tremendous artillery preparation and were reluctant to accept the enormous losses caused by the islets and the Spanish and German artillery. They had only been willing to sacrifice the punitive units. Moreover, the Soviet officers lost control of their soldiers in the looting and casualties suffered and, when they re-established command, they made the mistake of wasting time on the hedgehogs and with the isolated groups, instead of concentrating and continuing their advance. On the other hand, Soviet tanks, deprived of their infantry escort, hesitated to go further down Krasny Bor towards Sablino and Nikolskoye. All this allowed Reinlein, Bellod and von Bock to establish a line based on the artillery emplacements along the heights.

The early arrival of von Below ensured that the efforts of Bellod and von Bock were not in vain. It also allowed the SS Polizei Division to change fronts and entrench themselves. And it is clear that, if Heckel had acted with the same decisiveness as von Below, there would have been a better chance of saving the heights of Krasny Bor.

The combination of Russian errors and strenuous Spanish resistance bought time for the 18th Army and 50th Army Corps to send powerful forces into this vital sector. Every minute of profit was paid for at a very high price. Almost two thousand two hundred Spanish casualties cost those precious hours. The Battle of Krasny Bor was over, but the 55th Red Army had only stumbled, not been stopped.

On Thursday morning, General Esteban Infantes, who had returned from Prokovskaia, sent his daily report to the Military Attaché in Berlin, but as neither the General nor his General Staff really knew what was going on, the telegram was very confusing, as well as short: "The Division is engaged in hard fighting at Krasny Bor. His spirit is excellent. Our casualties were three killed and 10 wounded." But the message didn't reach Berlin until Friday, February 12. Bewildered, the Military Attaché decided to wait for more news, as the number of casualties did not square with an important action. A few hours later a new telegram arrived in which, after briefly describing the Soviet attack, he indicated the losses of three infantry battalions, two anti-tank companies, two sapper companies, and a cavalry squadron, as well as two artillery batteries. Obviously, the general was not yet in complete control of the situation. It also called for the immediate dispatch of two marching battalions (about 2,000 men), as well as replacements for six infantry commanders, an engineer commander, and a cavalry commander.

Stunned by the request for the urgent dispatch of personnel to cover casualties, Colonel Roca de Togores telephoned Madrid and, unable to communicate with the Chief of the Central General Staff, General García Valiño, asked to speak with the Minister of the Army, General Asensio, who patiently listened as the Colonel communicated the fragmentary message of Esteba Infantes. This message had been partially confirmed by the Russian news agency TASS and the British BBC. Likewise, Esteban Infantes reported that he had already alerted the 20th Marching Battalion, which was in Hof, with which he would cover half of the casualties, including some of the requested commands. General Asensio approved the measures and telephoned the Marching Battalion that was concentrated in Logroño, in order to speed up their preparations for departure for Germany.

When Robles was sent to undertake the reorganization of the 262nd, Colonel Rubio assumed command of the entire subsector of the Izhora. At the request of the Army Corps, Esteban Infantes opened an investigation into Colonel Sagrado's conduct at Krasny Bor and Colonel Kleffel opened his investigation into Colonel Heckel's conduct. Sagrado was relieved and sent to Spain and Heckel was sent to the reserve.

While Rubio and Cano clung to the Izhora and Lieutenant Colonel Robles reorganized the 262nd, Esteban Infantes tried to re-establish Spanish prestige. Lindemann and Kleffel discussed the February 10 performances. Kleffel heaped praise on the Spanish officers who had fought heroically, but on the other hand the command of the regiment was not energetic enough. The two generals agreed that, as long as the officers lived, the guripas had fought well, but the German command had long appreciated that the continual movement in the ranks, with novice troops, opened up the possibility of panic under artillery fire and sluggish attacks once the unity of command was broken. The next day Lindemann, in communication with the Army Corps, praised the Spanish officers, with a special mention for the gunners.

On the same Saturday, Reinlein returned from Krasny Bor. He and his men had managed to save the German battery. Now, three days after the sector was handed over to the 212th Division, and forty-eight hours after it was ordered out, they were finally relieved. As the brave group gathered at the Prokovskaya maneuver field, fatigue and hunger were reflected on their faces. Disdain appeared on the faces of Reinlein and Andrés while, in a resting position, they were enveloped by the praise of Esteban Infantes. Their faces seemed to say, "Where were you, my General?" Seeking to gain prestige by association, Esteban Infantes awarded Reinlein a well-earned Individual Military Medal and appointed him his Adjutant.

But the German generals were not deceived. They knew that the chiefs and officers, and not the division command, were the ones who had triumphed. All of Kleffel's apprehensions when Muñoz Grandes' departure was revived. Von Küchler and Lindemann discussed the withdrawal of the Blue Division from the front and its dispatch to Novgorod. General Esteban Infantes was traveling back and forth with his new Adjutant, desperately hoping to regain respect. Instead, the Germans placed the 170th Division behind their line.

On February 20, Esteban Infantes assigned Lieutenant Colonel Robles, another of Krasny Bor's heroes, to command the 262nd Regiment.

On the afternoon of the same day, the Military Attaché received a report in Berlin specifying that the total number of Spanish combatants in the Battle of Krasny Bor had been 4,200 men and that their losses had amounted to 53%.

The arrival of the 20th Marching Battalion allowed Esteban Infantes to cover about half of his casualties. At the front, there were only patrol clashes, raids and routine artillery shelling, although air activity and vehicle traffic in the Kolpino area continued to be intense.

With the arrival of spring and the rise in temperature, the roles changed again, this time for the last time. The Russian offensives lost steam and the Wehrmacht began its attack plans again.

On 14 March, von Küchler transmitted to Lindemann a directive from the OKH for which Operation Parkplatz. A defensive phase was envisaged for Army Group North, in which the liberated divisions of Demiansk would be reorganized and reinforced as attack divisions. Another unit would also be prepared for the attacking division: the 250th Division or Blau Division. Everything had to be ready for July. Parkplatz required two stages: an advance to Lake Ladoga would re-establish the site, and then the city of Leningrad would be stormed.

On the 16th, Lindemann went to Pokrovskaia to confer with Esteban Infantes, although he had previously conferred with Knüppel, the Chief of the Liaison Detachment, who advised him that if there was a difficult order, it would be best for him to sign it personally, which indicated that the Spanish general did not get along well with General Kleffel. no doubt as a result of the Battle of Krasny Bor.

Three days later, on the 19th, and at dawn, it seemed that Krasny Bor was going to be repeated: intense artillery fire, aerial bombardment, tank movement in Iam Izhora and fulminant destruction of communications. But fortunately, the artillery fire would not last long and was concentrated on the Spanish artillery rather than on the front line. When the infantry charged Robles' forces at Podolovo and Putrolovo, they were engulfed in a veritable deluge of shrapnel. Again and again, they launched the attack against the 1st and 30th Battalions of the 262nd, commanded by Commander Castro and Captain Calvo. Desperate to get the Moscow-Leningrad road opened before the rasputitsa (muddy conditions due to weather) turned the surrounding swampy terrain into a sea of mud, the Russians managed, for a short time, to overwhelm the outposts along the road, but the 3rd Battalion counterattacked and, in hand-to-hand combat, repulsed the Red Army's 72nd Division. Captain Merry Gordon was wounded, but by midnight hundreds of Soviet soldiers were hanging from the barbed wire, the Izhora being secured. Under the able command of Lieutenant Colonel Robles, the 262nd had once again become a fearsome fighting unit.

For its part, the Russian 55th Army also failed to move eastward and cut off the Sablino-MGA road. Robles, Bellod and Castro had conscientiously fulfilled their duty and together they returned to Spain, at the beginning of April, with the 11th Return Battalion.

Lieutenant Colonel Villegas joined the Division's General Staff at the beginning of April and officially replaced Colonel Andino on April 10. By this time the Division, with the arrival of the 20th and 21st Marching Battalions, had brought the Division's strength to 15,025 men, but its artillery had not been complete as the Germans were short of artillery pieces.

The 2nd Infantry Brigade of the Waffen SS still remained on the left of the Division at Aleksandrovka, while the 254th Division of the Wehrmacht covered the Red Forest on the right.

By the end of May, all units of the Division were practically at 100% strength, although many of the newly arrived "mortadella" had only three weeks of training. The 23rd Marching Battalion, commanded by Commander Gueda, was composed mostly of members of the 1st Line of the Phalanx, but nevertheless about 15% of its personnel were Guripa veterans who had decided not to repatriate and to remain in Russia for another year.

In those last days of May, Esteban Infantes was promoted to General of Division and received a visit from the Chief of Staff of the Army, General Martínez Campos, who had traveled to Germany. On the afternoon of June 1, Marshal von Küchler returned to Army Group Headquarters in Pskov from the "Wolf Burrow," where he had had had a tiring but exhilarating day.

The Blue Division was preparing for the attack, more chiefs and officers arrived and so on June 14 Colonel Navarro took charge of the General Staff of the Division and Colonel Amado of the 263rd regiment, then Lieutenant Colonel Villegas became second in command of the 263rd. But no sooner had Amado taken command at Pushkin than the Soviet 56th Infantry Division attacked.

After months of quiet, the Russians were back in action. On June 17, five companies, at 2:30 a.m., attacked, taking advantage of the darkness and throwing smoke screens. An intense artillery fire fell for thirty minutes on the positions of El Dedo, of the 262nd, and El Alcázar, of the 263rd, preceding the assault of their infantry. But the Spanish artillery immediately began shelling the Red concentrations. The Russians were advancing under a curtain of fire and managed to briefly break through the trenches, but an hour later it was all over. The greatest effort had been made against "El Dedo", leaving one hundred and thirty dead of the punishment company that began the assault lying on the ground and hanging from the Frisian horses in the Spanish trenches.

On July 18, General Esteban Infantes, on the occasion of celebrating the seventh anniversary of the National Uprising, prepared a party to which he invited Generals Lindemann, Kleffel, Eberhard Kinzel (Chief of the Northern Army Group), Hans Speth (Chief of the 18th Army), Walter Krause (of the 170th! Division) and Friedrich Köchling (of the 254th Division). The General shone as he led his brilliant guests into the park of the palace, where the months full of excellent delicacies and wine from Spain had been set up. Everything was going smoothly. At the end of the second course, Esteban Infantes got up and praised the Germans, but when Lindemann got up to answer him, it seemed that the sky was coming down on them. Dozens of Russian 122-gun guns were gunning down Pokovskaia. Esteban Infantes sat paralyzed as clouds of dust, shock waves and shrapnel helmets covered everything. The generals were looking at each other, a few seconds passed and Esteban Infantes met his gaze with Lindemann and there was an imperceptible nod and they all rushed to the basement of the palace to jump into the trenches opened last April. The honor guard, made up of frontline veterans, did not wait for the order and immediately sought shelter. Some of the E.M. officers were wounded, and Alemany, caught in the head, was killed. The banquet turned out to be a failure. Kleffel was not satisfied, for he had drawn the conclusion that the Russians had been informed and that they would try, another day, to destroy all the commanders of the Army, so he immediately ordered the construction of well-protected shelters in all the alternative headquarters.

Soviet power was growing and Allied pressures were mounting, so General Franco began to consider withdrawing the Division. The outcome of the Battle of Kursk and the fall of Mussolini on July 25 were decisive. The Spanish press began to shift to a neutral stance. On July 29, Franco received a visit from Carlton Hayes, the American ambassador, who unequivocally recommended that he declare neutrality before long, and was satisfied with Franco's reply.

But on August 29 Samuel Hoare, the English ambassador, also met with Franco, who listened calmly, but without being convinced. Bewildered and annoyed at not being able to get Franco into any of the ties he laid for him, he flew to London and in an explosive interview with the BBC and Allied press correspondents, stated that he had imperatively asked him to withdraw from the Blue Division. The Spaniards were rightly enraged and Jordana, Minister of Foreign Affairs, summoned Ambassador Hayes to tell him that Hoare had complicated the departure of the Division, since it could be understood as forced and not voluntary, so delays would be caused. On September 9, Soviet loudspeakers, manned by Spanish Republican exiles, broadcast the last Allied communiqués and in front of the position of the 10th Company of the 262nd, in Aleksandrovka, a huge sign written in red appeared: "! Spaniards, Italy has capitulated! Switch over to us!" Enraged by this comparison with the Italians, Colonel Valcárcel's guripas slipped up to the Russian barbed wire fences and smashed the offensive poster. A few hours later another advertisement appeared, this time in the Spanish trenches, proudly proclaiming: "We are not Italians!".

Repatriation

Rumours of a possible return of the Division increased when the decision finally came on 24 September at a meeting of the Council of Ministers, at which Francisco Franco announced that the Spanish Division of volunteers was going to return and that it would be replaced by a Legion. Although what was discussed in the Councils of Ministers is considered secret, moments after the end of the council the German Ambassador Dieckhoff already had the information of what was discussed in his possession.

But Franco did not achieve anything until October 1, when he officially declared neutrality. On the 2nd, Vidal, the Ambassador in Berlin, was instructed to inform Hitler of the Spanish government's intention to withdraw the Division. The Spaniards were facing the rudos, but surrounded by the Wehrmacht and some in Madrid were uneasy about what Hitler might do, but Hitler ordered that the men of the 250th Division should be treated with the utmost respect.

Late on the night of October 4, 1943, the Army Corps suddenly notified the General Staff of the Division to communicate that General Lindemann would arrive the next morning, in order to impose the Knight's Cross on General Esteban Infantes. Surprised by this hasty ceremony, the M.E. wondered what it was all about. Thus, at 10.15 a.m., Lindemann arrived accompanied by General Wilhelm Wegener, who had just replaced General Kleffel, who was not in good health, in command of the Army Group. At the end of the ceremony, Lindemann asked Esteban Infantes about the morale of the Division and he replied: "Morale is good, my General, and losses have been low, only three hundred men in the past three months." The head of the Liaison Detachment, Knüppel, listened attentively. He knew that the Spanish General had not yet been informed. The Army Corps had called the night before to inform them that the Division was to be withdrawn from the front line for further training, without Esteban Infantes imagining that he had been deliberately deceived, since Lindemann knew perfectly well, from the OKH, that the 250th Division was returning to Spain. Esteban Infantes' voice interrupted. The Russians had made another attempt and again had been repulsed.

Captain Morón had just arrived with the 26th Marching Battalion and was assigned to the 269th, where Cano entrusted him with the command of his 9th Company, with positions in the Poshinskii-Central sector, east of Slavianka. Suddenly, at 4:45 a.m., artillery, mortars, and anti-tank guns began pounding the positions of the 9th Company. After an hour and a quarter of the bombardment, two companies of the 3rd Battalion of the 213th Infantry Regiment emerged from the darkness and launched the attack through the open corridors in the Spanish barbed wire. The guripas watched Captain Morón and wondered how he was going to react. He tried to call the 269th, but the lines were cut, so taking his MP-8/41 he opened fire on the shadowy figures advancing on the ground and no man. The veterans were pleased and felt better. Although new, the Captain was one of his own. Morón was not without luck, since his section chiefs were very veteran and, aware of the Guripas' penchant for persecution, they led them in a clean-up operation. They counted twenty-five Russian dead, including the Commander-in-Chief of the 3rd Battalion who had refused to surrender. Later, when the fog lifted, the Spaniards counted up to 40 pairs of stretcher-bearers who were dedicated to removing the wounded. Spanish casualties were only eighteen.

When Esteban Infantes spoke enthusiastically to the German generals about how the "Ivans" had been repulsed, he noticed that Lindemann seemed somewhat reserved. When he finished his story, Lindemann announced that the 250th Division would be withdrawn from the front to rest and receive later training, which pleased him, since the Division had been at the front for two years and he had also requested that the new recruits undergo a period of training and moreover, there were rumors of an oncoming offensive against

Oranienbaum's pocket and with his men rested and well prepared, he hoped to end his destiny as head of the Division with a victorious offensive.

The withdrawal began on the night of 7-8 October. The five reserve battalions (1st and 3rd of the 262nd; 2nd of the 263rd and 1st and 2nd of the 269th) began their long march west on the muddy and half-icy roads to Volosovo and Nikolaievka. The battalions of the line remained until the 170th Division was able to move east. On 12 October, a Spanish national holiday, Soviet artillery went into action and their 189th Division attacked the salient still defending the 2nd of the 262nd, but they were repulsed after suffering heavy casualties. On that same day, General Esteban Infantes, still without officially knowing the withdrawal of the Division, handed over command of the sector. The Junkers Ju-52 liaison had not arrived.

At three o'clock that same afternoon, Lindemann, after having received orders from the OKH, went to report Esteban Infantes to Nikolaievka. There, in the presence of Reinlein, Knüppel and Metternich, he gave him the news of repatriation. He, like the others, was dumbfounded. Perplexed and embarrassed, Esteban Infantes asked for time to contact the Military Attaché in Berlin.

On November 7, Esteban Infantes was received by Adolf Hitler to say goodbye, but Hitler did not tell him anything about the repatriation of the Division, since all these details concerned Marshal Keitel.

The reception that was being given in Spain, to the veterans who were arriving in the different expeditions, was cold and the official receptions were furtive and subdued, since Franco did not want to publicize the withdrawal. By 16 November, a total of 3,347 men had returned to Spain.

The following day, the General Order of the DEV No. 69 was published, establishing the Spanish Legion of Volunteers (LEV). In reality, it constituted a regiment with three Infantry Battalions and oneself, with a total of 2,133 men. Colonel Navarro was appointed to his command.

On 13 December, the last remaining Spaniards left Russia: the quartermaster's staff, transports and staff of the 31st Relief Battalion. In the USSR there remained the Blue Legion, which only remained until the beginning of March 1944, as we will learn in the next chapter.

On December 12, 1942, General Muñoz Grandes was ordered to return to Spain, despite significant opposition from the Germans to his departure. And two days later Adolf Hitler imposed the Oak Leaves on his Knight's Cross of the Order of the Iron Cross, which he already owned. The command fell to the until then second in command of the Division, General Emilio Esteban Infantes Martín, who would later also receive the Knight's Cross of the Iron Cross.

▲ Countryside Mass for DA men (NEG).

▲ Arrival of General Muñoz Grandes at the Estación del Norte in Madrid on 18 December 1942 (LET).

▼ General Muñoz Grandes reviews the troops to be repatriated after their hard stay on the Russian front (LET).

▲ General Muñoz Grandes smokes a cigarette on his way to greet the first group of DEV returnees. The cold Soviet climate is felt in the Spanish locker room (LET).

▼ Another moment of the first repatriation of the division's first group of soldiers in March 1942, in which General Muñoz Grandes personally participated with the DEV leadership (LET).

▲ The time of departure approaches and the men crammed into the wagons look out to see their commander, General Muñoz Grandes (LET).

▼ General Muñoz Grandes was always highly appreciated by his men, as can be seen in the photo in which he greets the first group of volunteers returning to Spain after serving for 7 months on the Russian front (LET).

▲ Farewell between comrades before leaving for Spain after remaining on the Eastern Front (LET).

▼ March 1942. Several divisionaries cannot hide their joy at the imminent return home, despite being crammed into the railway carriages that will take them to the rear (LET).

▲ The good mood of the Spaniards was maintained on many occasions despite the circumstances during their stay on the Russian front (LET).

▲ The Divisionaries on their return to Spain are assisted by female Nazi party personnel (LET).

▼ Colonel Pimentel's return to Spain after his stay in the DEV (LET).

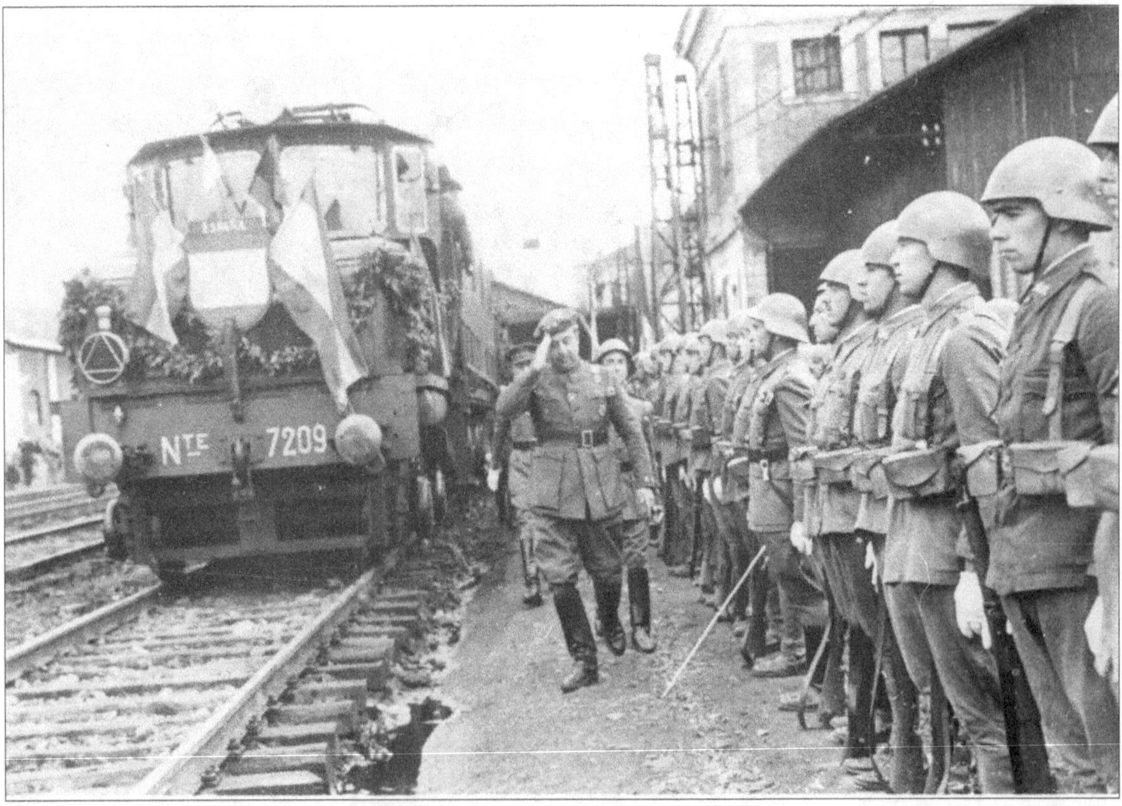

▲ Return of Colonel Pimentel, commander of the Wehrmacht's 262nd Infantry Regiment of the 250th Infantry Division, with his men on 24 May 1942 in Irún. Pictured receiving a bouquet of flowers from Celia Jiménez, godmother of the DA (LET).

▼ Parade of a group of ex-divisionaries after their return to Spain from the Eastern Front (LET).

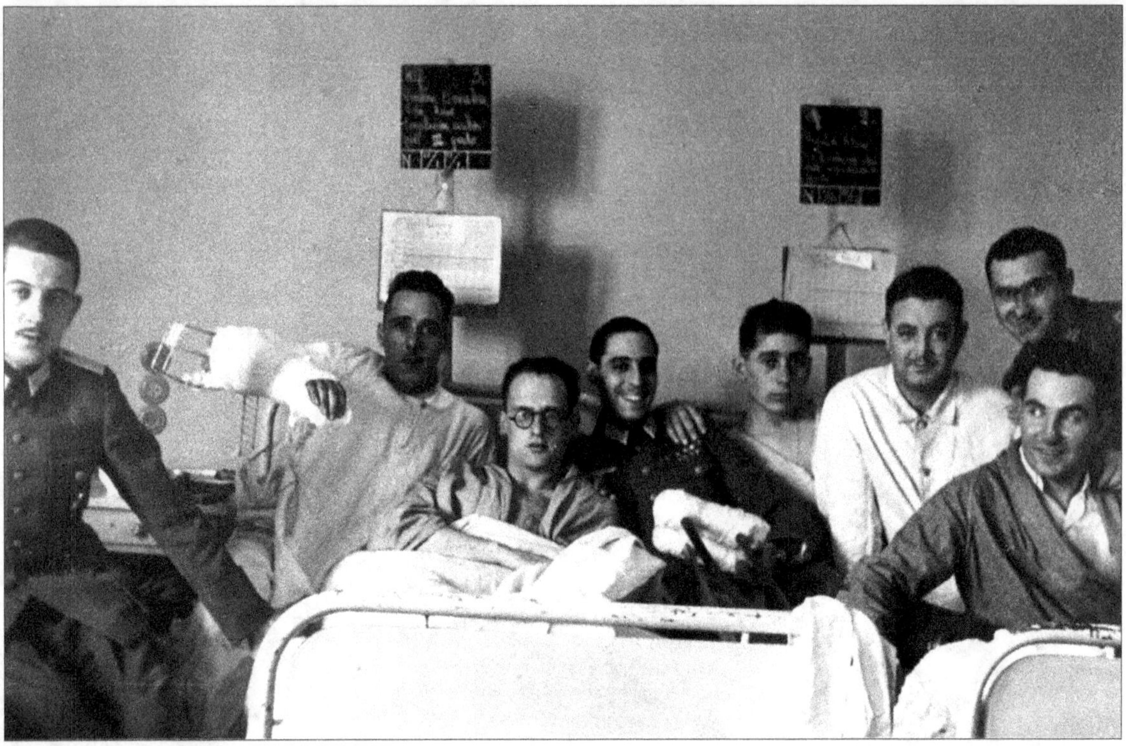

▲ Wounded DEV soldiers pose for the photographer in a hospital (LET).

▼ DEV soldiers injured in Maudes Hospital in Madrid (LET).

▲ The cadet knights of the Toledo Infantry Academy wear a mixture of Spanish and German decorations on their uniforms (LET).

▲ This proud veteran of the Russian front displays a mixture of German and Spanish insignia (LET).

▼ Three DEV veterans attend lectures at the Complutense University in blue shirts with the Wehrmacht eagle, the Iron Cross 2nd class and other Spanish insignia (LET).

▲▼ Farewell to a battalion of returnees by General Muñoz Grandes (BVD).

▲▼ Farewell to a battalion of returnees by General Muñoz Grandes (BVD).

▲ Portrait of Lieutenant Colonel Zamalloa, accompanied by a group of members of the medical corps of the Blue Division, gathered in a train carriage at the time of departure for Spain (BVD).

BIBLIOGRAPHY

Ailsby, C. Hell on the eastern front. The Waffen SS war in Russia. 1941-1945. Brown Packaging Books Ltd. 1998.

Alcaide, J. A. Berlín a muerte. Revista española de historia militar. Nº 10. Quirón Ediciones. 2001.

Antill, P. Berlin 1945. End of the thousand year Reich. Osprey Publishing. 2005.

Archivos del Ministerio de Asuntos Exteriores.

Arráez Cerdá, J. Les espagnols de la Wehrmacht. La División Azul. Ciel de Guerre 19. 2011.

Bajo las banderas del III Reich alemán. Españoles en Rusia, 1941-1945. Defensa. Mayo 1999.

Beevor, A. Berlín 1945. La caída. Memoria Crítica. 2002.

Berlin 1945. Magazine 39-45. nº 82. Hors-Série Historica. 2005.

Berlin 1945. Magazine 39-45. nº 83. Hors-Série Historica. 2005.

Biddiscombe, P. Los últimos nazis. El movimiento de resistencia alemán 1944-1947. Books4pocket 74. Inédita Ediciones. 2008.

Bishop, C. Hitler´s foreign divisions. Foreing volunteers in the Waffen-SS 1940-1945. Amber Books Ltd. 2005.

Bowen, Wayne H.: «The Ghost Battalion: Spaniards in the Waffen-SS, 1944-1945», The Historian, vol. 63 (2001).

Boyle D. La II guerra mundial en imágenes. EDIMAT Libros S.A. 2000.

Bueno, J. M. La división y la escuadrilla azul. Su organización y sus uniformes. Aldaba militaria. 2003.

Caballero, C. División Azul. Estructura de una fuerza de combate. Galland Books. 2009.

Caballero, C. Carlomagno. Voluntarios franceses en la Waffen SS. García Hispán. 2003.

Caballero, C. División Azul. Estructuira de una Fuerza de Combate. Galland Books. 2009.

Caballero, C. La División Azul. La Esfera de los Libros. 2019.

Caballero, C; Guillén, S: Las escuadrillas azules en Rusia, Almena, Madrid, 1999.

Caballero, C. Morir en Rusia. La División Azul en la batalla de Krasny Bor. Quirón Ediciones. 2004.

Caballero, C: El batallón fantasma. Españoles en la Wehrmacht y Waffen-SS, 1944-45, CEHRE y ACTV, Alicante-Valencia, 1987.

Caballero, C: Los últimos de los últimos. El batallón fantasma. Extra nº 53. Revista Defensa.

Caballero, C: Waffen-SS. Los centuriones del III Reich. Extra nº 21. Revista Defensa.

Cardona. G. El gigante descalzo. Aguilar. 2003.

Darman, P. Uniforms of world war II. Blitz Editions. 1998.

Davis, B. L. German army. Uniforms and insigniia. 1933-1945. Brockhamptom Press. 1992.

De Caixal, D. Waffen SS. Los templarios de Hitler en combate. Almena. 2003.

Escuadra, A: Bajo las banderas de la Kriegsmarine. Marinos españoles en la Armada alemana, Fundación Don Rodrigo, Madrid, 1998.

Ezquerra, M. Berlín a vida o muerte. García Hispán. 1999.

Fernández, F. Carros de combate y vehículos acorazados alemanes. Servicio de publicaciones del EME. 1988.

Fey, W. Armor battles of the Waffen SS. 1943-45. Stackpole Books. 2003.

García, A M. "Galubaya Divisia". Crónica de la División Azul. Fondo de Estudios Sociales. 2001.

García, M. Semíramis, 1954: El regreso de los cautivos de la División Azul. Nº 46 Revista Española de Historia Militar.

Gil Martínez, Eduardo Manuel. Españoles en las SS y la Wehrmacht. La unidad Ezquerra en la batalla de Berlín 1945. Almena. 2011.

Gómez, M S; Sacristán, E. España y Portugal durante la Segunda Guerra Mundial. Espacio, Tiempo y Forma. Serie V. Hª. Contemporánea, nº 2, 1989, págs 209-225.

Gómez, M S. España y Portugal ante la Segunda Guerra Mundial desde 1939 hasta 1942. Espacio, Tiempo y Forma. Serie V. Hª. Contemporánea, t 7, 1994, págs 165-179.

González Pinilla, A. La División Azul en el periódico Enlace. Gutiskland. 2018.

González Pinilla, A. La Legión Clandestina. Gutiskland. 2021.

Hamilton, A.S. Bloody Street. The Soviet assault on Berlin. Helion. 2020.

Heiber, H. Hitler y sus generales. Memoria crítica. 2005.

Holzträger, H. In a raging inferno. Combat units of the Hitler Youth 1944-45. Helion. 2000.

Jacobsen, HA. Dollinger, H. La Segunda Guerra Mundial. Volumen octavo. Plaza & Janés Editores S.A. 1989.

Keegan, J. Waffen SS. Los soldados del asfalto. Editorial San Martín. 1979.

Kent, C; Wolber, T; Hewitt, C. The Lion and the Eagle: German-Spanish Relations Over the Centuries ; an Interdisciplinary Approach. Berghahn Books, 1999.

Kleinfeld, G. Tambs, L. La división española de Hitler. La División Azul en Rusia. Editorial San Martín. 1983.

Kurowski, F. Hitler´s last bastion. The final battles for the Reich. 1944-1945. Schiffer Military History. 1998.

L´agonie du III. Reich. 1945. Berlin. Batailles & Blindés Hors-Serie nº 1. 2005.

Lagarde, J. German soldiers of world war two. Histoire & Collection. 2005.

La Segunda Guerra Mundial. Victoria en Europa I. Time Life Folio. 1995.

Lehmann, A. En el bunker de Hitler. Testimonio de un niño soldado que vivió los últimos días del Führer. Editorial El Ateneo. 2005.

Loringhoven, B. F. En el bunker con Hitler. Booket. 2007.

Lumsden, R. SS Regalia. Grange books. 1995.

Mabire, J. Los Waffen SS franceses. Los últimos defensores de Hitler. Biblioteca Nacionalsocialista Iberoamericana Volumen V. 2003.

Martínez Canales, F. Lenigrado 1941-44. Almena. 2009.

Mitcham, S W. German order of battle. Volume two. Stackpole Military History Series. 2007.

Mollo, A. The armed forces of World War II. Uniforms, insignia & organization. Greenwich Editions. 2000.

Morales, G; Togores, L E. Las fotografías de una historia. La División Azul. La Esfera de los Libros. 2008.

Moreno, X. Legión Azul y Segunda Guerra Mundial. Actas Editorial. 2014.

Moreno, X. La División Azul. Sangre española en Rusia, 1941-1945. Booket. 2006.

Muñoz, A. Göring´s Grenadiers. The Luftwaffe Field Divisions 1942-1945. Axis Europa Books. 2002.

Nart, J. El Jefe español de las SS. Interviú núm. 339, Madrid, noviembre de 1982.

Norling, S E. Guerreros de Borgoña. Historia de los voluntarios valones de León Degrelle en el Frente del Este. El ocaso de los Dioses (1944-1945). García Hispán Editor. 2008.

Norling, S E. Raza de Vikingos. La División SS Nordland (1943-1945). García Hispán Editor. Segunda Edición.

Norling, S E. The story of a Spanish Waffen SS-Officer. SS-Obersturmführer R. Luis García Valdajos. Siegrunen 79.

Núñez Seixas, X M: «¿Un nazismo colaboracionista español? Martín de Arrizubieta, Wilhelm Faupel y los últimos de Berlín (1944-45)», Historia Social, 51 (2005).

Pallud, JP. Parker, D. Volstad, R. Ardenas 1944: Peiper y Skorzeny. Ediciones del Prado. 1994.

Pérez, C A. Españoles en la Segunda Guerra Mundial (I) Combatiendo por el III Reich. 2006 (texto en internet).

Pérez, Manuel; Prieto, Antonio. Legión Española de Voluntarios en Rusia. Los últimos de la División Azul. Actas Editorial. 2014.

Peterson, D. Waffen SS Camouflage Uniforms & Post-War Derivates. Windrow & Green Ltd 1995.

Puente, M. Yo, muerto en Rusia. Memorias del Alférez Ocañas de la División Azul. Editorial San Martín. 2003.

Recio, R. Españoles en la segunda guera mundial (el frente del este). Vandalia. 1999.

Recio, R. González, A. Uniformes del ejército de tierra alemán. Heer 1933-1945. Euro Uniformes.

Recio, R; González, A. Das Heer. Uniformes y distintivos. Agualarga. 1996.

Ryan, C. La última batalla. La caída de Berlín y la derrota del nazismo. Salvat.2003.

Simons, G. La Segunda Guerra Mundial. Victoria en Europa I. Time Life Folio.1995.

Sourd, Jean-Pierre. True Believers. Spanish Volunteers in the Heer and Waffen-SS, 1944-1945, Europa Books, New York, 2004.

Sourd, Jean-Pierre. Croisés d´un idéal. Dualpha. 2007.

Torres Gallego, Gregorio. El gran libro de Diccionario del Tercer Reich. Tikal. 2009.

Torres Gallego, Gregorio. «Españoles en las Waffen SS. Italia, 1945», Revista Española de Historia Militar, nº10. 2001.

Trevor, H. R. Los últimos días de Hitler. José Janés Editor. 1949.

Tusell, J. Gran Crónica de la Segunda Guerra Mundial. Volumen 16. Edilibro. 1945.

Vadillo, F. Los irreductibles. García Hispán. 1993.

Waffen SS. Los centuriones del Reich. Defensa. Febrero 1993.

Westwell, I. Brandenburgers. The Third Reich´s special forces. Ian Allan Publishing.2003.

Williamson, G. Las SS: Instrumento de terror de Hitler. Ágata. 2002.

Williamson, G; Andrew, S. The Waffen-SS (4). 24 to 38 Divisions & Volunteer Legions. Osprey Publishing. 2004.

Ziemke, E. F. La batalla de Berlín. Fin del Tercer Reich. San Martín. 1982.

WEBSITES

web www.agrupacion1seis.com

web http://er.users.netlink.co.uk/biblio/ibarruri/armando.htm Política exterior franquista y la Segunda Guerra Mundial por Armando López Salinas

web www.exordio.com

web www.forosegundaguerra.com

web http://greyfalcon.us

web http: //groups.msn.com/memoriadivisionazul/general.msn

web www.gutenberg-e.org

web www.hispanismo.org

web www.history.navy.mil/library/online/germandefberl.htm

web www.historynet.com

web HistoriasigloXX.org

web www.lssah.es

web http://memoriablau.foros.ws

web www.militar.org.ua

web www.mundosgm.com Forum.

web http://www.theeasternfront.co.uk

web usuarios.lycos.es/jnroldan/index.htm

web http://visantain.iespana.es/

web http://wikanda.cordobapedia.es

web Wikipedia. Varios artículos.

web www.ww2f.com

web www.zweiterweltkrieg.org Forum.

TITOLI GIÀ PUBBLICATI - TITLES ALREADY PUBLISHING